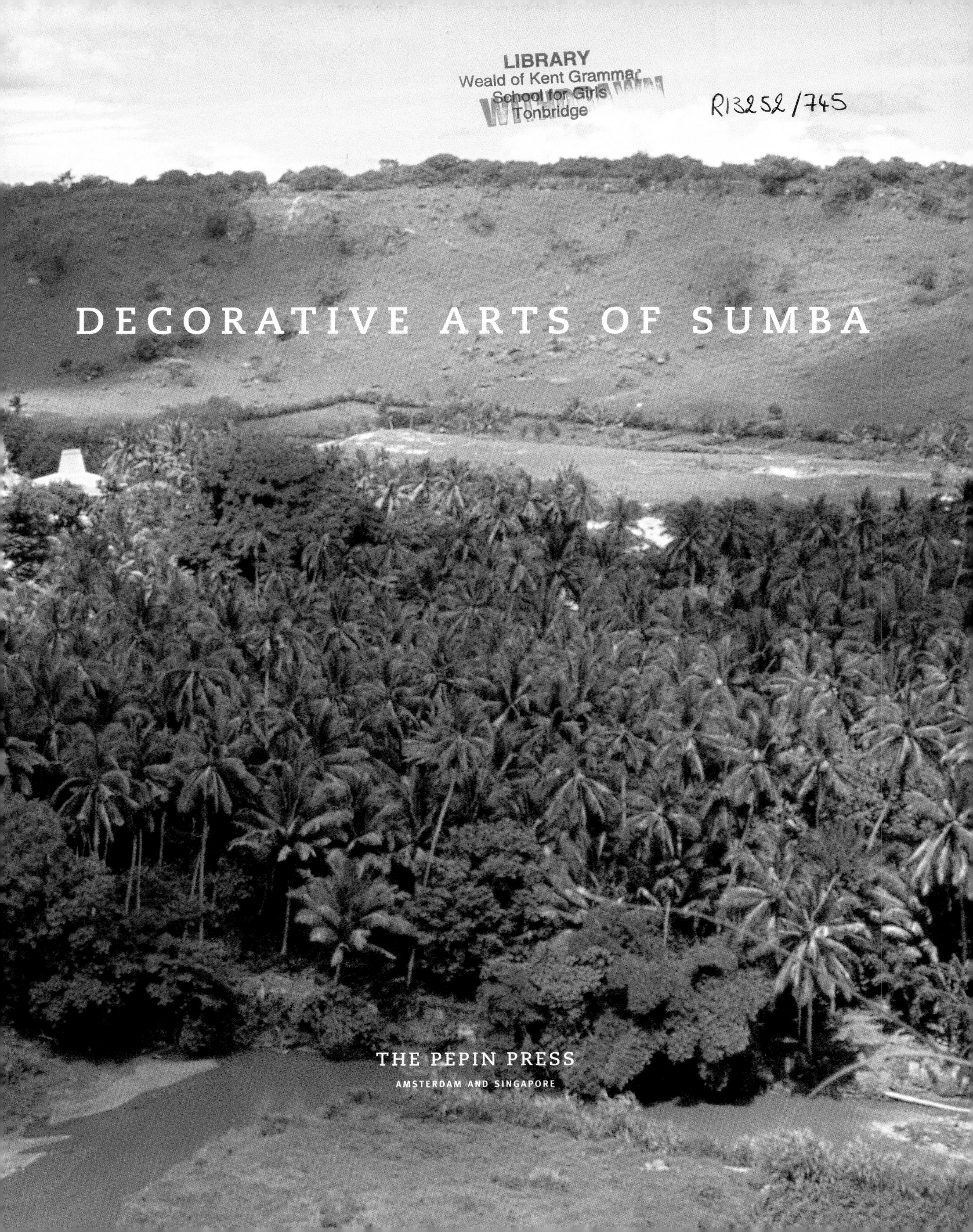

DECORATIVE ARTS OF SUMBA

THE PEPIN PRESS

AMSTERDAM AND SINGAPORE

First published by the Pepin Press BV in 1999

ISBN 90 5496 050 7

A catalogue record for this book is available
from the publishers and from the Royal
Dutch Library, The Hague

This book is edited, designed and produced
by The Pepin Press in Amsterdam and
Singapore
Design: Dorine van den Beukel
Photography: Helma Bongenaar
(collection Museum of Ethnology Rotterdam)
and Wouter Thorn-Leeson
(reproduction B/W photographs)
English copy editing: Alison Fisher

The Pepin Press
P.O. Box 10349
1001 EH Amsterdam
The Netherlands
Fax: (+) 31 20 4201152
Email: mail@pepinpress.com

Printed and bound in Singapore

Page 2-3: Ratu Merapu alongside
a tombstone, c. 1960.
Page 1: Detail from the cloth illustrated on
page 84.
Page 4-5: Rende, East Sumba.
Page 6: *Lau pahudu*, woman's sarong,
East Sumba, late 19th or early 20th century,
warp ikat and supplementary warp,
imported cotton yarn, 122 x 90 + 93 cm.
Page 8: Sumbanese couple, late 19th or early
20th century.

Contents

Foreword

The Museum voor Volkenkunde (Museum of Ethnology) in Rotterdam is internationally recognized for housing important collections of textiles originating from Indonesia. Several of the first directors of the institute displayed a keen interest in the textile art of the former Netherlands Indies and kept close ties with potential sources. Indonesian culture has always produced rich and varied textiles, and many historical examples are found in the collection of which we are justifiably proud.

In 1964 a recently graduated cultural anthropologist from Columbia University in New York, Marie Jeanne Adams, began studying Sumba in Dutch museums and other institutions. As she devoted much time to the textiles in our museum, it was decided to organize a major exhibition in 1965 based on her expert knowledge before she departed to take up fieldwork on Sumba itself. She was assisted in this endeavour by Alit Djajasoebrata, assistant curator of the Indonesia Department. A small brochure accompanied the exhibit under the same name: 'Life and Death on Sumba'. We thank Dr. M.J. Adams, now a renowned specialist in Sumbanese arts, for her graceful permission to reprint here a revised edition of the original text.

Much has changed since 1965, both in Sumba and in its surrounding world, and the time has come to focus on Sumbanese textiles once more. In this publication which we, in cooperation with the Pepin Press, are happy to present, we offer an insight into our splendid Sumba collection. Much remains to be discovered about the background and origins of our objects. It is our sincere hope that in future more aspects of the imaginative Sumbanese art can be revealed through research, and we hope that the illustrations in this book will inspire textile artists on Sumba as well as elsewhere.

Our special thanks go to the Archives of the Reformed Protestant Church in the Netherlands in Leusden, who courteously allowed us to choose freely from their extensive photo archive.

The contribution by Dr. Jill Forshee, who may be considered Dr. Adams' successor in Sumba studies, deserves appreciation. It is through her lively lines that the beautiful textiles and objects, so long kept in the museum vaults, obtain new meaning.

The other contributors to this volume are affiliated to various departments of our museum. I want to thank them and our curator Alit Djajasoebrata, for their contribution to both this publication and the exhibition.

Hein Reedijk
Director of the Rotterdam Museum of Ethnology

Life and death on Sumba

Marie Jeanne Adams
revised by Sandra van den Broek

Sumba, land of giant tombs and silent villages. Sumba, land of lively dances and colourful costumes. Such contrasts are natural to life on Sumba, an island in the eastern part of Indonesia.

The island of Sumba, occupying an area of 11,000 km^2, consists of large limestone plateaus covered with tough grasses and broken by sudden valleys and irregular hills. Thousands of wild horses roam in the vast grasslands of eastern Sumba. Horses and cattle are the major source of wealth for the nobility, as the exceptionally dry climate and stony ground are not good for agriculture.

Most of the people live widely dispersed on small farms and depend on the short rainy season to produce sufficient maize, rice and tubers to last through the year. The western half of the island receives enough rain to permit considerable wet rice farming and supports two-thirds of the population of approximately 500,000.

History

According to 14th-century chronicles Sumba was part of the great Majapahit kingdom that ruled a large part of the Southeast Asia islands from Java in the 14th and 15th centuries. In the 17th century the island came under the rule of Bima in Sumbawa and Goa in South-Sulawesi. However, the history of Sumba is mostly one of internal wars in which rival kingdoms fought over land and trade rights.

Although the Sumbanese shun the sea, many seafaring traders have regularly visited their shores. Sandalwood, horses and slaves were the main export products. In 1756 the Dutch United East India Trading Company (VOC, Vereenigde Oostindische Compagnie) signed their first trading agreement with the local rulers. Since trade subsequently suffered from the many internal wars, the Dutch invaded the island in 1906 to secure their economic interests. In 1912 a colonial government was installed which ruled the island through the Sumbanese nobility.

The Dutch conquest opened up another external market, one for the large, colourfully decorated textiles which were used by the Sumbanese as festival

Above: Sumbanese men, c. 1900.
Page 10: Old Sumbanese posing on a tombstone, c. 1960.

Dutch missionary travelling in Sumba, 1926.

clothing and as wrapping for the dead. By the beginning of the 20th century, these attractive cloths were very popular amongst western avant-garde art-lovers and were sold by fashionable department stores like Liberty's in London and Metz in Amsterdam.

With the installation of the Republic of Indonesia, the rule of the traditional aristocracy officially came to an end. However, as many noblemen became government officials, their families continued to exert influence and still are the major economic and cultural force in Sumbanese life.

Family, religion and gift exchange

The traditional religion, called Marapu, is still very important to the Sumbanese, and 27% (1995) of the population is officially registered as a follower of this religion. Even for the 68% Christians, the traditional beliefs, directions and rituals retain significance.

The traditional Sumbanese way of life binds family, religion and economics indissolubly together. The people belong to patrilineal clans, that is, groups of families who honour the same founding fathers. After death, these great men become *Marapu*; they become the invisible powers who can help (or if neglected, harm) their descendants. The Sumbanese man often turns to his Marapu for advice. He does this through prayer and by sacrificing a chicken and reading the intestines or by handling an oracle spear. This is done before starting on a trip, embarking on discussions on any matter of importance, beginning work in the fields, planting or harvesting, or in case of sickness. As one Sumbanese said, he could not give up his religion, as he would not know what was going to happen tomorrow or the day after tomorrow!

Several families of one clan may be spread over a district or be scattered over half the island. Families of different clans are linked by marriage ties. These widespread ties between blood relations and in-laws are important in the event of major festivals, gravestone dragging, or conflict, when both persons and goods from other districts may be needed. These ties were also important when bartering goods between the inland and the coastal districts. In former days food produce and goods could only be obtained as part of a ceremonial gift exchange between good friends and relatives. Although food and modern commodities can now be bought at the market, the important prestige goods, like quality textiles and golden objects are not sold. They are still part of the traditional exchange system based on clan affiliations.

The ceremonial centre

On the occasion of the many festivities that are held annually in both East and West Sumba, people come from their small farm settlements and gather at a central village in the district. This village, *praing*, is primarily a ceremonial centre rather than what we think of as a village. The praing are picturesquely situated on top of strategic hills. The location and the thick stone or cactus walls that surround it helped in the old days to defend it against enemy attack. This was very important, for within the praing the great men are buried, and the priceless heirlooms of important families are stored in the tall roofs of the sacred family houses.

Visually, the praing is an unusual place. In the central square stands a group of giant limestone tombs or gravestones which look like thick stone tables. Around the tombs, large square houses are raised on piles two metres above the ground; their tall peaked roofs tower 10 to 15 metres in the sky. This type of roof, characteristic of Sumba, is the most sacred part of the house. For instance, Umbu Ndilu, a hero in popular stories, puts on his magical, 'gilded' garments and turban in the attic, before going out to do the great deeds that will make him rich and famous.

Festivals

For most of the year, the praing is deserted. Other than a chicken straying across the square, a small child playing beneath a grave table, an old woman on a shaded gallery, no signs of life are visible: Sumba, the land of the giant tombs and silent villages. But in the festival time of the year, the scene changes, and the life amid these tombs is no longer dull. The houses fill up with families and their guests from nearby settlements. The central grave square becomes the scene of all kind of activities, both work and play.

The coverstones of the tombs are called not only *todina*, 'cover', but also *diru lodu*, 'basking in the sun'. Rows of holes are carved into the diru lodu for playing *motu*, a game of chance the Sumbanese are particularly fond of. At the grave square people gather and enjoy chewing *pahapa* together. Pahapa means simply 'something to chew' and refers to a quid of areca palm nuts, betel leaves, lime powder and tobacco, all of which has a mild narcotic effect. Over the broad surface of one tomb, a young girl will be turning rice sheaves to dry in the sun; on another, women dry their textiles. At a gathering, a particularly high tomb serves as a podium to seat those with high rank.

Overleaf: Sumbanese village with tombstones, c. 1960.

In the village square, people gather to welcome an important visitor, to celebrate a wedding or a funeral, or to honour the dead at the New Year's feast. On such festival occasions, besides feasting on plentiful meat and rice, the people sing, dance and engage in competitive games. In West Sumba, people come from far and wide to watch the *pasola*, a tournament in which two teams compete in throwing blunted spears at each other.

The women's dances include quick steps done while brandishing knives and also slow undulating movements of arms and neck that we usually associate with Hindu-Javanese styles. The men's dances are lively and vigorous and include mock battles. Leaders of the ceremonies and dancers, both male and female, are draped in beautifully decorated textiles. Gleaming gold ornaments hang from their foreheads and chests. Sumba is then the land of lively dances and colourful costumes.

Before and after planting rice, custom decrees sedate behaviour for all people. Feasts and fun are taboo. Once the rice is ripe, the season for noisy games begins, for the rice threshers' dance, for riddles, storytelling and singing. These activities are not only permitted, they are necessary. The harvest must be received with a show of joy, as a friend and companion, a guest and visitor who comes from afar and has reached his goal after a long trip. 'The words must be overflowing' they say, 'so that the food will be abundant'. After the harvest there are the top spinning games in the fields, where small teams compete in a kind of fertility rite for the next season.

Above: Sumbanese girl drying paddy on a tombstone, c. 1960.
Page 16: Sumbanese man with two boys, c. 1960.
Overleaf:
Page 18: Sacred dances at a rice ceremony, c. 1960.
Page 19: Harvest time, c. 1960.

Women's work, textiles

Between the happy occasions of festivals, the women work constantly. Besides helping in the fields and gardens, they pound the rice, grind the maize, cook the food and make the clothing. Weaving is a major occupation, but the colourfully dyed textiles are made only in certain districts, mainly the western and eastern littoral. In some parts of the interior, weaving is forbidden by the local *adat* (custom).

Sumbanese legends recount how a bundle of warp threads, only visible to the ancestors, ties the island to the sky and to the bottom of the sea. These threads cross the centre of the island and keep the land resting on the sea. Weaving wears down these warp threads and weakens them. Not only does it weaken the fabric of the weaver, but also that of the cosmic loom. Weaving therefore is not allowed in the centre of the island, where the cosmic warp is situated. The threads that hold the island could break, and the island would fall into the sea.

Left: Sumbanese woman weaving,
c. 1960
Right: Ikat loom, c. 1960.

For interest and variety of design, the traditional textiles of Sumba stand out from all others of Eastern Indonesia. They are unique because they employ bright colours and contain many animal, plant and human figures in a horizontal arrangement over the cloth. The costumes are not tailored garments but large, flat, rectangular cloths which are wrapped around the wearer. The Sumbanese man dressed in two of these wraps *hinggi kombu* – one around the waist and the other over his shoulder – and a large bright turban, he presents an impressive appearance.

To decorate an East Sumba *hinggi* calls for a long complicated process of dyeing, which the Sumbanese refer to as *kombu*. This is the name of the rust-red dyestuff drawn from the roots of the kombu tree *(Morinda citrifolia)*. The kombu colour is more highly prized than the other colour, blue *(wora)*, obtained by indigo dyeing. The textiles give an impression of many colours, but the Sumbanese only use indigo and kombu. Overdyeing and redipping create the vari-coloured effect. For the most part the designs appear in the natural colour of the cloth. The colours are applied to the warp (the lengthwise yarn) before weaving. This method of decorating by dyeing before weaving we call *ikat*, from the Indonesian word 'to bind'. On Sumba it is *hondu hemba*, warp binding. First, the women tie the pattern and the parts to be dyed rust onto the warp with dye-resistant bindings, such as strips made from lontar palm leaves, and dip the threads into the blue dye. Then they untie the parts to be dyed rust and put the warp threads through the complex kombu dyeing process. Formerly, a tan stain was painted on here and there after the cloth was woven, possibly as a way of gilding it. Only the women of the nobility and their servants know these decorating techniques. According to another Sumbanese legend, the island is a body with a woven covering, a 'skin' that lets rain through and protects the groundwater. The rain, often seen as the sperm of the male heaven, feeds the female earth and makes the plants grow. To prevent these fruitful juices from flowing away, the far ends of the island must be tied off. The women on the outside edges of the island are therefore obliged to make ikat textiles.

On the West coast, in the Kodi district, the decorated men's wrap (Kodi: *hanggi*) consistently appears with a blue background, and the designs exhibit a rather abstract character. Usually, we can recognize only *mamuli* (Kodi: *hamuli*): a piece of jewellery, preferably gold, used as an eardrop all over Sumba. It is omega-shaped, and at the lower ends small birds, apes or a mounted rider may be affixed. In earlier times, men also wore it. It is a treasured symbol, connected in some way to the forefathers.

Some of the most attractive works of art in Indonesian textiles can be found among the women's sarongs of Eastern Sumba. These sarongs or *lau* use the same animal, plant and human designs as on the men's cloths, but employ a greater variety of decorative techniques. The women may use different coloured threads in the weaving, or make designs on the cloth with beads and shells. The type called *lau pahudu* is exceptionally beautiful. In the central band of the skirt, figures are woven in a light coloured thread against a dark background. This is an extra thread, in addition to the basic weave (warp and weft), and appears on the surface just to form the figures. The formal directness and colour contrast of the *pahudu* technique heightens the arresting quality of Sumbanese designs.

Sumbanese woman with *mamuli*, c. 1960.

The Sumbanese and their possessions

The association of women with textiles is more than a simple division of labour. The Sumbanese classify textiles as 'feminine' goods. So are beaded bands and jewellery, porcelain and pigs, which the women look after. 'Masculine' goods consist of the larger livestock, that is, karbow and horses, and of metal work, such as gold, silver or copper ornaments, spears, swords, and gongs. These objects are not only sacred but represent the major forms of wealth within the traditional culture.

In the traditional beliefs of Sumba, objects and animals are not just impersonal possessions. They have their own 'force'. The Sumbanese therefore feel a close bond with their possessions. When a man loses his *pahapa* sack, his shoulder cloth or his knife, he feels powerless and prays for the return of his 'life force'. The owner of a brave spiritual horse is proud to be known far

Sumbanese women, c. 1960.

and wide by his horse's name. After the karbow are made to work, trampling his fields, a special rite is performed to 'cool their feet' and restore good relations between man and beast. The Sumbanese can only eat meat if the animal has been slaughtered by the proper person employing particular actions and prayers. If a person acquires much wealth quickly, he may die young, overwhelmed by the 'life force' of his possesions. At the same time, abundant wealth belongs to the greatest good, to what the Sumbanese call, 'all that is cool and fresh'.

Marriage

Marriage has always been a major occasion for the exchange of goods, and sets up a pattern of exchange between the families that can last for generations. A traditional *adat* marriage is the subject of a great deal of discussion for months, even years, within the family group. When a young man is ready to marry, a *wunang*, or speaker, approaches the bride's family with a 'masculine' gift, that is, a mamuli and a horse. The gift is called 'the flag which stirs the heart, the bird's crest which disturbs one within'.

If the proposal is acceptable, the bride's father replies with a 'feminine' countergift of textiles: a man's hinggi and a woman's lau. This exchange is equivalent to a marriage contract, but months of haggling will follow over the quantity and quality of the bride price, during which the bride's uncle will visit the family of the groom to examine the gifts being offered. These gifts must be of a 'masculine' character, that is, mamulis and other gold ornaments, spears, swords, horses and karbow or, in more recent times, a bicycle. According to the adat, eight pieces (eight, the perfect, fulfilling number) are to be exchanged on each side, but among the nobility, the gifts acquire an expensive character, amounting to many thousands of dollars, and payment may drag out over years.

On the day of the wedding, a party of the groom's relatives come to pick up the bride. All the bride's people leave their village and put up a mock fight. Their opposition is overcome by liberal gifts. In the bride's house, thirty or so women are singing. She sits among them, wrapped in six or seven decorated lau, her head covered with a tall hat and a textile which hangs over her face. Again there is a fight, this time between the groom's party and all the women. The men carry off the bride to a place outside the village where a feast is held for all the relatives. The groom's party then conducts the bride and her countergifts to their village. The gifts she brings are 'feminine': pigs, decorated and heavily beaded lau, ivory bracelets and bead jewellery. When she arrives people throw rice at her, and the groom's parents look over the gifts she has brought. The respect she receives from her in-laws will depend initially on the quality of her countergifts.

Festivities continue for several days, but all the while, the groom remains invisible. Finally, the bride is carried around the village, and the people of her party and the villagers throw things at each other. After that, the bride is taken in to meet her husband, and the marriage is concluded.

One of the strange and fascinating customs on Sumba is the use of the *ana mamosa*, a young girl who stands in for the bride. Through the long wedding ceremonies, the bride moves about freely, while the ana mamosa stands motionless wearing the heavy, richly decorated bridal costume and jewellery. She goes to the bride's new home as a kind of lady-in-waiting.

Traditional practices at weddings and funerals are still very much alive today among the Marapu believers as well as the Christian population. Sometimes traditional and Christian elements are combined, sometimes separate ceremonies are held on different days. Practices vary widely between villages.

Burial

When a man of the nobility dies, the corpse is wrapped in dozens of the finest textiles; gold chains and jewellery are tucked into the cloths. Before he can be buried, all family disputes must be settled; this may delay the funeral for several years. The wife's family has to see that the funeral includes abundant food for feasts and a suitably lavish display of wealth, including textiles and jewellery. This display assures the husband of entrance into the community's soulland.

At the funeral, a figure similar to the ana mamosa appears, wearing heavy, decorated lau and a tall hat and veil. Now she is one of the four *ata papangga*. All four, two men and two women, are richly costumed and decorated with gold chains and ornaments. The men wear golden karbow horns on their foreheads. Prior to the burial, they serve as personal attendants for the dead prince. One leads his favourite horse to the grave for an hour every day at sunrise and sunset. Another carries the special funeral pahapa sack, made of beads. They make daily food and pahapa offerings and guard the body. Perhaps, once again, the ana mamosa substitutes for the prince's wife.

On the day of the burial, the women gather in the nobleman's house to wail, and the men sing of the path the nobleman's ancestors took from their heavenly origin to their arrival on Sumba and the subsequent trek over Sumba to their present village. Women perform dance steps with his hinggi wrapped around their shoulders. The deceased's favourite mount leads the funeral cortege, and a servant holds a parasol over the horse's back to protect the

invisible rider from the sun. They are followed by the huge textile bundle containing the corpse. The ata papangga, 'those who are made to walk', act as if lifeless; they have to be supported. For a while, they are laid beside the open grave. In their trance-like state, they accompany the dead prince on his way to the soulland. One or two of his favourite mounts are stabbed and released to run off to die and to join their master in the heavenly village.

'The dead follow the way of the ancestors', the Sumbanese say. The rites are intended to prevent the soul from getting lost on its way back to the heavenly village in the sky. Without this ritual, the soul strays and goes to the sun or stars. Only after much prayer and costly ceremonies can it be called back, to send it off again on its proper way. Once the nobleman reaches the heavenly village, he is in a position to help his descendants. Their prayers can reach him there; if called upon, he can return to his family house.

After the death of a friend, a Sumbanese man may strum his *jungga*, a two-stringed lute, and improvise mourning songs:

I am a horse running alone,

I am a man standing alone,

a lost yelping dog,

a buffalo who can find no water,

a horse in a lonely valley.

I feel like someone

who goes to the edge of an abyss,

who walks across a swaying tree trunk

above a wild and streaming river.

Ana Kami, my companion!

Closed are your eyes,

Fallen is your horse.

I raise my voice to speak,

You are silent and do not answer.

I raise my voice to speak,

Answer me, you who sit

on the unmoving stones [the living humans]

on the dry land.

Answer me, you who sit

in the rocky caverns

in the deep water. [the dead]

I sit still and listen

Give me answer and speak.

Page 24: Old Sumbanese man, c. 1960.
Overleaf: Tombstone in Anakalang, c. 1960.

Skull tree in Lewa, East Sumba, c. 1960.

The crowning glory for a Sumbanese is to receive a great tombstone, erected by his family after his death. The stone is cut from the native limestone of the island; in some areas this is so soft when first uncovered that it can be chopped with an axe. Many of these gravestones weigh ten tons, and some are as large as 30 tons. Here again, the relatives of the wife and the husband share the responsibility of gathering the hundreds of men required to drag the immense stones by ropes to the hilltop village. Tremendous amounts of food are needed to feed everyone, and the history and greatness of the dead man's family are repeated over and over in all-night recitations and songs.

House building

Building a house is a major undertaking for the social group. It is not a task for a small, new family as it requires great wealth and much cooperation from many friends and relatives. Exchange of gifts and provision of ritual meals, consisting of karbow meat and rice, accompany every phase of the building. The house is essentially a covered platform, built around four main posts. Procuring these posts, which sometimes measure over a metre in thickness, in wood-poor Sumba is a difficult and expensive process. The roof, consisting of bamboo slats, rises in two stages. One part begins at the outer edge of the floor and slants upward to the top of the four main posts. Above the posts, another bamboo framework rises steeply and meets at the top pair of ridgepoles, 15 to 20 metres off the ground. Bundles of grasses, tied over the entire roof, shade the galleries surrounding the house.

The family spends its day not in the dark interior but on the galleries. There, guests receive generous hospitality which always includes food and pahapa. On the broad galleries, women plait baskets, make pottery, set up their loom; men beat barkcloth, decorate small containers with attractive figures, carve curved knife handles or mend their fishing nets.

The interior space is divided into male and female halves. The men's section is across the front. Their space is used for family discussions and religious ritual. In the back, alongside the kitchen and food storage, there is a room devoted to the former head of the family. His pahapa sack hangs there, and an older woman supplies offerings and prayers to his spirit. The upper beams of the house are covered with carvings. They serve as offering places for the several patron spirits of the family. In the attic under the tall roof, the family heirlooms and altar to the oldest family gods are housed. In the family house as in the village square, there is a striking mixture of activities of the living and the dead. The past and those who once lived in it are kept in close contact with the living community.

Marapu statue, c. 1960.
Mostly a marapu is a standing stone, in this case, it has the shape of a man.

Headhunting

Nowhere this interplay of ideas about life and death is so evident as in the custom of headhunting which came to an end early in this century. In the centre of an important village, the *andung* (skull tree) stood – a tall dead tree set in a pile of stones, holding on its bare branches human skulls, captured in open warfare or by stealth from enemy districts. Women and priests remained in the village during the headhunting, and complicated rites were required for cleaning the heads and purifying the warriors before they could re-enter the village. The scalps were especially sacred and were fastened to swords or kept in the sacred attic. The skull tree represents the death of the enemy and therefore the security of the village. For the Sumbanese, it was also the centre of religion and necessary for the proper unfolding of the seasons, the coming of rain and the fertility of the land. Nowadays, the andung is one of the intriguing motifs on the textiles of Sumba.

Unfolding passages:

weaving through the centuries in East Sumba

Jill Forshee

Unfolding through the century

In this last decade of the 20th century, the vividly graphic fabrics of eastern
Sumba remain integral to local society, while incorporating numerous modern and international influences. Locally produced textiles reflect profound
changes that have taken place on the island over the century, as they continue to carry ancient images. The island of Sumba has become world
renowned through its textiles, gold items, and megalithic funeral markers.
Tourist guidebooks and travel accounts describe Sumba as a remote and wild
place within Indonesia, somewhere between the lavish culture and comforts
of Bali and the 'primitive' dangers of Irian Jaya. Images of dramatic rituals, a
rich material culture, and unchanging, 'traditional' ways of life have increasingly drawn international tourists and collectors of non-Western art to the
island. Yet, the people of Sumba have never lived isolated or frozen in time,
and their traditions have continuously transformed to include changing
views and circumstances.[1]

Sumbanese fabrics have always been in some kind of motion – most obvi-
ously on the bodies of people who wear them, but also in passages from one
stage of being to another, such as marriage or death. Textiles have long indi-
cated – visibly – human comings and goings, while asserting identities, con-
veying meanings, and tracing numerous social interactions throughout the
island's past. In the motifs and compositions of eastern Sumba's fabrics are
the woven poetics of how history has affected the people who produce,
trade, and wear them. At the same time, cloth embodies innovative forces
always inherent in the forms and events by which time is measured.

Significant European influences began to pervade eastern Sumba through
Dutch missionaries and colonial officers in the early decades of the 20th century. After World War II (and the end of the Dutch colonial presence), Sumba
was one of thousands of islands across a vast archipelago which came to be
included within the new nation of Indonesia under Sukarno. Following this,
a state bureaucracy was established on Sumba, agricultural development
projects were set in motion, and an educational system sponsored by the
new Indonesian government spread throughout the island. Along with pres-

Rende, East Sumba.

Ikat clad Christ beckons from the front of
a Catholic church in the town of Waingapu,
East Sumba.

sures upon the Sumbanese to send their children to school came stipulations
from the national government involving religion. New ideology was set forth
in 'Five Principles' (*Pancasila*), the first of which proclaimed belief in one
Supreme Deity. Local people were encouraged to convert from their historical animist belief system (*Marapu*) to a world religion recognized by the government centered in distant Jakarta.

A number of Sumbanese had previously converted to Christianity through
the influences of former European missionaries and their schools.[2] While the
majority of converts on the island were to follow some form of Christianity,
others converted to Islam (the majority faith of Indonesia). These latter converts had largely married into Arab families in the port town of Waingapu, or
into Muslim families who had migrated to Sumba from other Indonesian
islands, such as Sulawesi, Java, and Flores. It is difficult to say exactly what
percentage of Sumbanese were within the folds of monotheistic religions by
the second half of the 20th century, and this would vary considerably in different regions of the island in any case. Forth estimated (in the 1970s) that
despite several decades of missionary efforts, the majority of Sumbanese,
probably more than two-thirds in East Sumba, still retained their traditional
religion. During my research period in the early 1990s, I estimated this percentage as roughly half of the population. All such approximations, however,
are dubious, as many Sumbanese (succumbing to government pressures)
claim to be followers of Christianity while still carrying on with Marapu
beliefs and practices. Adherence to Marapu customs (*huri marapu*) is especially resilient as it involves relative social status, marriage, and death rituals. Textiles are crucial to all of these concerns.

Imposed educational and religious institutions had become well-established
in eastern Sumba by 1980, although many village people in the region also
continued with much of their former way of life. It was around this time that
international tourism to the region began to increase appreciably. As air service developed to Sumba from Bali, it became a possible stop on a holiday
tour of Indonesia, and eastern Sumbanese people grew accustomed to seeing
all manner of strange, foreign visitors entering their villages. Tourism was
sometimes greeted with mixed responses, however, as certain villages had
been depleted of some of their finest heirlooms (cloth, gold, and even funeral
stones) through the 1960s and 1970s. While some of this transfer occurred
through the willing sale of objects by locals to agents of a foreign market,
according to many people in East Sumba, this period was also marked by the
theft of precious articles. In addition to valuable personal possessions
(*banda*), the sacred property of ancestors (*tunggu marapu*) disappeared from
Sumbanese homes and graves. Today, eastern Sumbanese people are often
ambivalent in their accounts of how the world has come to know and pos-

sess their arts. A lively current market surrounds the production and trade of the region's fabrics and has stimulated a vibrant resurgence in design and quality in many instances. Nonetheless, narratives of loss and theft can be heard on village porches, as people tell of the appropriation of their 'possessions of beauty' *(banda hamu)* by foreign collectors.

Bound and mobile

The eastern Sumbanese have been producing, wearing, and trading for centuries a kind of cloth now known internationally as *ikat* – which is uniquely pictorial and extremely complex in the making. *Ikat* means 'to bind' in the Indonesian language, which describes the basic process in the production of the fabrics (referred to in the eastern Sumbanese language of Kambera as *hemba hondu*, meaning 'bound cloth'). This involves the patterned binding – the tight wrapping with strips of dried palm frond – of selected bundles of the warp yarns before weaving to create a resistance to the dye bath.

Fabrics from East Sumba have historically been major prestige markers for the noble caste, and their exchange substantiates alliances between clans. Cloth also carries cosmological symbolism based in local animist concepts. The Marapu belief system basically structures the universe in complementary dualisms – male/female, hot/cold, sweet/bitter, etcetera (as generally do all indigenous cosmologies of eastern Indonesia).[3] The well-being of the people complexly entwines with the good will of the ancestors (also called *Marapu*), who are propitiated by offerings, rituals, and daily practices. In Sumba, everything seems to be regarded as possessing spirit *(ndewa)*, a certain life force that might thrive or sicken depending upon earthly or metaphysical influences. Environments or states of being are often characterized as hot *(mbana)* or cool *(maringu)*. Coolness is a desired quality, and often rituals are held in order to offset the dangers of a spiritual heat – a condition of wild places or an affliction caused by improper behaviour. Various sorts of spirits, including those of animals, inhabit Sumbanese cosmological worlds and might assist or afflict humans. Textiles in eastern Sumba are crucial in Marapu rituals which aim to balance universal forces, and colourfully enfold people as they move through the passages of life.

Although widely collected by the Dutch prior to Indonesian independence and long prized in international textile collections, in the last decades of the 20th century foreign demand for Sumbanese fabrics has increased immensely due to the international tourist trade in Indonesia. This trade is centered largely on the island of Bali, but has also stimulated growing numbers of tourists to venture to Sumba. Following this trade in recent times, thousands

Above: Nobleman, tombstones and clan home in the village of Rende.
Below: Modern tombstone next to satellite dish. New and old prestige symbols coexist in many Sumbanese villages.
Overleaf: Sumbanese horseman.

Above: Ikat warp before being dyed.
Below: Ikat warps ready to be woven
after dyeing.

of Sumbanese textiles have entered the commodity flow of a global ethnic arts market, and their motifs have been absorbed into an international design pool. Images from Sumbanese textiles now grace coffee cups in California and stylish jackets on Paris streets.

The present noble caste (maramba) on Sumba still possesses the expertise and resources to produce fine weavings, and thus continues to enjoy the status of owning the best of the island's fabrics. New forms of prestige, however, have joined the tableau of Sumbanese status symbols, and these are associated with demonstrating connections with outsiders and travelling away from the island (most frequently to the other Indonesian islands of Bali and Java, several hundred kilometers to the west of Sumba) to participate in the internationalized textile trade in cosmopolitan centres.

Currently in eastern Sumba, there are numerous ironies and tensions between the historical and the innovative, as people in villages respond to a multicultural world, made more immediate to them by the greatly expanded trade in local textiles. While modern, international influences have had the effect of diminishing the quality and local meaning of textiles in many cases, these same external forces have also stimulated tremendous creativity on the part of East Sumba's designers, weavers, and traders – producing a revival in cloth production and various transformations in people's lives. Such creativity, moreover, has long been a mechanism through which people in Sumba have taken account of themselves in the world, in the face of multiple foreign influences. Sumbanese textiles carry inventiveness and lore, as they move through the hands of merchants who expedite their exchange as international commodities. Following the routes of world trade, the fabrics eventually come to adorn walls and bodies in regions far from their sources.

Values, methods, contexts

Upon entering any of the weaving villages of eastern Sumba, a visitor will likely witness a scene typical of textile production. Women of all ages sit on porches of the high-peaked ancestral houses (uma kabihu) and weave (tinungu) threads coloured with local plant pigments, or bind (pahondu) warps with strips of palm frond to resist certain dyes, and occasionally take breaks to chew betel nut (pahapa) and chat. Funerary stones (watu reti) often loom several yards away from many such houses, carved with animals, human figures, and geometric symbols similar to those woven into local textiles.

Indigo (Indigofera sumatrana, L.) grows wild in eastern Sumba, although some regions cultivate it. Fermented leaves are reduced to a paste in water, and when mixed as a dye bath, indigo gives textiles their distinctive blue colour.

The area for indigo dyeing in any particular household is isolated, customarily, well away from the home. Usually women past the age of child-bearing engage in this process, their hands and forearms stained a blackish blue as they lift skeins of cotton threads from the pungent baths. For the Sumbanese, indigo dye *(wora)* is surrounded by perils. A bulbous, blue dye pot sitting at the edge of a yard effectively enforces gendered prohibitions and fears that are part of the lore and alchemy surrounding the indigo plant and its liquids. Indigo often evokes feminine body fluids and the dangers and moral symbolism associated with them.[3] The hazards borne by such liquids and the importance of binding yarns tightly to resist fluids (or keep other essences in) is a correlation that emerges in the cited studies and in my own. The elusiveness of body fluids and of dyes characterizes elements that uncontrollably flow between realms, through earth, air and water. Eastern Sumbanese speak in whispers of the curses that might be carried in small amounts of menstrual blood or liquid indigo – both of which are substances employed in local sorcery *(marungu)*. This malign magic is taken very seriously in eastern Sumba, and men are frequently most fearful of it. In the 1990s, I knew of a number of cases of male illness, impotence, or madness which were blamed on female sorcerers, and the afflicting essences involved were those just discussed.

The other main dye pigment long employed in Sumbanese cloth is called *kombu* after the tree it is taken from (the inner bark of the roots of *Morinda citrifolia*, L.). This produces a hue ranging in tone from rust to bright red, depending upon the addition of a mordant known as *loba* (from the bark of the tree *Aleuritas moluccana*, L., candlenut in English). Red relates to social rank and is historically a colour limited to nobility. Women (and sometimes men) pound the *kombu* bark, and eventually dip yarns into the resulting red dye bath. *Kombu* is usually applied after indigo. Although dyeing in Sumba has customarily taken place at specific times of year relating to harvest cycles and the availability of dye stuffs, following the currently accelerated rate of textile production in eastern Sumba, dyeing often proceeds year-round.

Eastern Sumbanese prize complex designs, with intricate, curving forms that are difficult to render using the ikat method. They also value deeply saturated colours, achieved through repeated immersions in dye baths. Although many commercial pieces now use expedient chemical dyes, the better fabrics achieve their quality through the skillful and time-consuming use of the leaves of the indigo plant and roots of the kombu tree. These pigments not only render the deep blues and reds typical of East Sumba's fabrics, but when dyed one upon the other produce richly muted secondary colours such as wine, brown, or purple. Muddy colours are not admired and are referred to scornfully as *nda nabara*, meaning 'not clear' or 'dirty'. The number and clarity of the finished hues reflect the exhaustive binding and unbinding involved in creating a multicoloured cloth.

Textile production has maintained a certain division of labour between men and women in Sumba, and although today the rare man can be seen weaving for the commercial market, women still largely produce the cloth. In villages, men often sit in family compounds and tie or untie bound bundles of yarns before and after dyeing, or twine the unwoven end of warp threads of a cloth after completion (a process called *kabakil*).

Less typical of Sumbanese environments of textile production than the scenes depicted above (and more likely to escape the eyes of foreign visitors to the island) are the growing numbers of shops and small factories that currently produce textiles for a tourist and export market. In commercial towns, Sumbanese weavers often work sequestered in the back rooms of various shopkeepers and exporters, who then sell the fabrics in numerous art shops (in Sumba and in tourist towns of Bali) as traditional village cloth. Moreover, Sumbanese village women now often toil on a piece-work basis for town merchants, producing textiles in their homes for low pay; fabrics which will immediately enter the inventory of outside entrepreneurs after completion.

This loss of control over the creation and profits from fabrics is at the centre of numerous laments in Sumbanese villages, and people especially denounce entrepreneurs along ethnic or religious lines, accusing Indonesian Chinese or Muslim merchants of appropriating local fabric designs along with village labour. Indeed, Sumbanese villagers carry on their own discourses of authenticity regarding fabrics – criticizing textiles that are poorly executed or reproduced by non-Sumbanese. Cloth produced by other than indigenous people is often derided as Chinese cloth *(hemba tau Hina)* or Arab cloth *(hemba tau Arab)*, labelling the fabrics as mere facsimiles of genuine Sumbanese textiles.

Fabrics continue to figure prominently in eastern Sumbanese life and rituals

and are often central in status competitions between people. Many textiles are created specifically for local purposes, and even those produced for the outside market will frequently be worn or displayed by villagers prior to their sale. The blanket-sized cloths familiar to many foreigners are made to be worn by men. Called *hinggi*,[4] the cloths are folded, cinched, and draped on the body to resemble something between an Indonesian *sarung* and a Scottish kilt. They are also worn as shoulder cloths. Essential in marriage exchange, such textiles travel with a bride to her husband's village as part of her nuptial agreement. What is more, a demonstrated skill at creating cloth persists as a requisite for women marrying into a number of eastern Sumbanese villages.[5]

Social organization in East Sumba, as in other areas of eastern Indonesia, has historically been manifested through exchange relationships based on marriage.[6] The movement of brides and cloth between villages substantiates this on a basic level. Marriages are frequently complex, long-negotiated agreements between clans and necessitate the exchange of textiles *(hemba)* by a woman's kin (wife-givers, called *yera*) and gold items *(banda amahu*, or gold wealth) and livestock *(banda luri*, or living wealth) by a man's family (wife-takers, called *ana kawini*). Life-long obligations continue between these clans, with the wife-givers generally enjoying higher status than their counterpart clan and being privileged to make claims for assistance from them in future rituals and times of hardship.

Upon death, a Sumbanese of high rank may be wrapped and buried in over one hundred *hinggi*, which will protect the soul from malevolent forces and identify the deceased (by motifs, colour, and quality of the outermost fabric) to ancestors in the next world. A village funeral *(taningu)* in Sumba may draw hundreds or even thousands of guests, with the women of each kin group contributing several woven textiles to the family of the deceased. Attendance at these events and the associated prestations of fabrics are considered crucial in maintaining social harmony – in both an everyday and supernatural sense.

Left: A group of women arriving at a funeral. The first woman is carrying textiles. Right: A fabric-draped coffin is carried to its grave.

Half of a *hinggi* on a loom. The other half is being woven in the background. Eventually the two halves of woven cloth will be sewn together up the middle to produce a large textile that mirrors itself from side to side.

Woven images

Historically, textiles of East Sumba reflect the dualistic conceptual basis of the Marapu faith. Designs are repeated both side-to-side and end-to-end, containing motifs which are richly symbolic of clan, rank, gender, and ancestral affiliation. These fabrics are the most boldly graphic of any textiles produced in eastern Indonesia – with numerous recognizable creatures and forms. Perhaps for this reason, they are especially popular internationally.

Distinctive motifs from eastern Sumba include the skull tree (*andung*), with its origins in the days when head-hunting was part of warfare between village domains. This motif has been configured into something resembling family crests by village households, and is especially prominent in the Rende region. Headhunting has long been outlawed in Sumba, first by the Dutch and then by the Indonesian authorities. Symbols such as the *andung*, however, continue to evoke tales of male prowess and the power of particular clans. Bühler (1955) suggests that Sumbanese skull tree motifs took their original design from older tree motifs general to the region. The tree in similarly symmetrical forms is seen throughout Southeast Asia.[7]

In current times, following decades of avid collecting by Westerners and Japanese, many eastern Sumbanese are well aware of the value foreigners place upon 'primitivism' in their quests for non-Western arts. People knowingly play on such romantic views, and the skull tree with its associations for foreigners of primitive ferocity is currently one of the most popular motifs in textiles created for a tourist market. In recent times, the motif has also made its way onto business cards and T-shirts of village entrepreneurs.

Animals in Sumba are symbolically and substantively connected with social status, wealth, and the passing of time (Hoskins 1993). The magnitude of public festivals in East Sumba is always reckoned by how many tails *(kiku)* are involved in the slaughter to feed guests. Moreover, through their exchange, animals mark the worth of women as part of the bride price *(wili tau)*. Animals connect and define people, viscerally, with higher powers and with each other. They sometimes also elicit affection. A man may be given the name of his horse, in addition to his personal name (Onvlee 1980a:196). Through animals, people in Sumba ponder their fates, devise their identities, and demonstrate their standing. All of these concerns are reinforced through fabric motifs.

Horses *(nyara)*, which in Sumba denote wealth, mobility, as well as male bravado, commonly animate textiles from the southeastern region of Mangili. In the early 20th century many Sumbanese became wealthy through the breeding of horses for sale to the Dutch cavalry (Onvlee 1980a). Horses also accompany departed souls to the next world (an ancestral realm called *awangu*, roughly analogous to the Western notion of heaven), and a horse is frequently sacrificed in eastern Sumba at funerals of high-ranking people.[8]

Chickens *(manu)* are popular motifs throughout East Sumba, and it is through augury *(uratu)* involving the entrails of these creatures that many people persist in attempting to make contact with their ancestral spirits, for guidance in this world. Such fowl, especially cocks, wield a vigilant power as well, standing atop homes, graves, and looming in the upper design fields of fabrics, heralding arrivals of what is as yet unseen by humans.

Aquatic and amphibious animals such as crayfish *(kuru mbia)*, turtles *(tanoma)*, and crocodiles *(wuya)* all relate to noble ranks and often denote personal qualities such as cunning, longevity, dualistic powers, and transformation to the next world. The crocodile (frequently claimed as an emblem of young noblemen) has the amphibious ability to live in (and often mediate between) two worlds – that of land *(tana)* and that of water *(wai)* – and, as such, is seen as powerful in more than one realm or mode of being. The vil-

Above: Skull trees, birds and crocodiles on a *hinggi* from Rende.
Centre: Angels from a Dutch children's bible on a *hinggi* in Prailiu.
Below: Dragon motif from Chinese porcelain.

Tourists examining a *hinggi* with pictures of the Dutch Queen Wilhelmina (1880-1962) as a motif. This has been a popular motif for decades and is an example of how foreign power becomes incorporated into eastern Sumbanese iconography.

lage princes of Sumba have long been the adventurers of their communities, those most motivated to form alliances with outside forces, while continually reasserting power within their village domains. As such, they have functioned in multiple realms, seeking prestige and identity by their dexterity in moving between worlds.

Indeed, a factor in the marking of high status for the Sumbanese has long been evident through various trade links and alliances with foreign powers. For centuries such associations occurred involving Indian, Arab, Portuguese, Dutch, and Chinese traders, as well as people from other islands of the Indonesian archipelago. As emblems of particular and prestigious alliances with outsiders, East Sumba adopted motifs from such powers into its own royal regalia.[9] In this way, foreign regal symbols such as the Dutch coat of arms, *patola* designs from Indian trade silks, and dragons from Chinese porcelain were borrowed, innovated upon, and incorporated into Sumbanese aesthetic fields. In turn, such symbols became a part of local traditions, while embodying a certain flux.

A forward facing human figure (called *tau*, meaning 'person' or sometimes referred to as *manuhia*, meaning 'humanity') is one of the oldest motifs to consistently appear in eastern Sumbanese fabrics. Similar figures appear in cloth from across Indonesia, and some scholars have considered these as descended from Dongson cultural migrations from Vietnam in past millennia.[10] In Timor, Flores, Kalimantan (Borneo) and other islands of the Malay-Indonesian archipelago, such figures are composed of geometric diamonds, triangles, and meanders and are abstractly recognizable as human forms. In Sumba, the figures exhibit explicitly more personality. Although formulaic in design, they are expressive in postures and details, often complete with internal organs and facial expressions. If such figures did indeed evolve from shared ancient sources, then the Sumbanese versions appear to have become considerably more animated (revealing a spiritedness the eastern Sumbanese call *hamangu*) than comparable ones from neighbouring regions.[11] Before Dutch colonists outlawed the practice earlier in this century, people below the rank of nobles were forbidden (under penalty of death) to wear fabrics and motifs which were the sumptuary privilege of royalty (Adams 1969). Currently, under an Indonesian state system, the historical nobility no longer has legal control on the island. The commodification of textiles – traditional prestige markers of the East Sumbanese nobility – through the general population has motivated regional elites to seek other status symbols not readily accessible to most people on Sumba. This has intensified a historical tendency to value alliances with outsiders and the material indicators. Such alliances, as in times past, have been largely forged through the travelling activities of young, elite men.

The dry season each year (the time between October and January, called *ndau wandu*) weighs heavily upon eastern Sumba in its relentless heat and shortage of food supplies. Noblemen and their servants have historically ventured out during this period, in a kind of travelling known as *mandara*, searching for food and beneficial exchanges with people of other regions. It is often during these months before the rains that traders nowadays travel away from eastern Sumba to distant Indonesian islands to sell their cloth.[12]

Indeed, travel itself, a certain going about (*halaku*), has become a prestigious symbol of modern mobility for many Sumbanese sojourners. There are, however, serious perils associated with travelling, such as death or illness away from home and the absence of family and protective spirits. Death away from home is especially unfortunate, as many in Sumba believe that the soul (*ndewa*) will wander lost thereafter. With whatever prestige venturing to far-off places may bring, a haunting tension between moving about and staying in place also follows people who leave the island. Moreover, independent ventures consistently challenge values in East Sumba that emphasize conduct in the service of the clan group and ancestors.[13] As people move away from their island more frequently, they encounter ideas and develop identities that conflict with Sumbanese customs. Some are better able than others to balance multiple moral worlds, and time can only reveal the lasting effects of this on communities in the region.

Regional market in the dry season.

Shifting positions

Along the paths of the production and trade of textiles on Sumba, one can get a palpable sense of what have been historically male (*mini*) and female (*kawini*) domains, as well as the role gender plays in determining mobility. Loom-bound women often appear in Sumba as stationary fixtures on village porches and have been traditionally discouraged from venturing outside of family compounds unescorted or without specific family matters to attend to, such as funerals. Villagers widely believe that women travelling alone are either the carriers or victims of black magic (*marungu*). Sumbanese will go to great lengths to avoid a woman given to sorcery, walking many kilometres out of their way to avoid passing through the village of a suspected witch.

The production of cloth in eastern Sumba substantiates a culturally ideal disposition of women as they work in family compounds. A circularity of the life cycle – birth, reproduction, and death – is metaphorically contained in the continuous warp in the process of becoming cloth on simple, backstrap looms. The tautness or laxness of this 'becoming' is entirely controlled by the weaver's body. Women are literally tied to their yarns as they embody

the looms they weave upon – their legs providing the tension of the warp, their backstraps securing them to the entire apparatus. Eastern Sumbanese say that women are instrumental in the flow or disruption of social life. The weaver engaged in the ongoing production of tightly woven cloth is an archetype for female conduct in general.

Much of the everyday discourse of social life goes on between women in their domestic spaces, often as they engage in binding, weaving, and dyeing processes. From the aeries of their elevated porches, women exchange tales, jokes, complaints, and general social commentary which sets the tone for village life in East Sumba. Working incessantly (and sometimes passionately) on their bound, dyed, and woven creations, women often fix the rest of the world within their own particular visions.

While they frequently guard older family motifs, some women improvise or reinterpret designs. Currently, certain households are reclaiming or reinventing specific motifs as their own, or combining techniques and images in new ways. Supplementary warp (pahikung) and ikat methods are sometimes seen together in inventive and striking manners, bringing prestige to the women who create such fabrics. While often sold to foreigners at relatively high prices, these textiles are also valued for family use.

In some villages, the outside market has stimulated a recent revival in the creation of lau hada, a woman's tubular skirt, graphically decorated with shells and beads. A particularly female discourse often underscores meaning attached to fabric designs, and a motif which men might reckon to represent the supernatural bestowal of power upon a standing male figure, women may whisper to allude (humorously) to castration. In this way, contested, multiple, or mutable meanings become apparent, within what surfaces as a push and pull between men's and women's worlds. In eastern Sumba, motifs in textiles evoke arguments as often as they do shared meanings between people.

What is more, people in eastern Sumba are increasingly knowledgeable about outsiders' notions of the 'tribal' or the 'primitive', and indeed, many have seen themselves depicted in Western museum literature in such terms. Through their frequent and ongoing interactions with foreigners, some villagers in Sumba possess catalogues from Western museums and galleries, which feature arts from so-called 'tribal' or 'primitive' regions of the world. Inspired by these now globally popular images, people currently include motifs in their fabrics for sale to outsiders that more closely resemble those from other Indonesian islands or even regions of Oceania or Africa than they do conventional Sumbanese designs.

Above: *Pahikung* weaving, supplementary warp, Rende.

Page 44: *Lau hada*, women's tubular skirts with figure motifs of shells and beads.

Left: Eastern Sumba ikat cloth inspired by an Australian catalogue on textiles from Borneo.
Right: Narrative cloth on which the story of a battle unfolds. Events proceed through time from the top to the bottom of the textile.

Movements in cloth

In the early 1980s, hinggi designs began to appear in eastern Sumba which no longer mirrored themselves bi-facially end-to-end (with largely floating, symbolic designs), as did regional cloth to that point. These new textiles told particular stories from top to bottom, inviting their display in full length. Hanging from trees or fluttering from village porches, these peculiar fabrics conveyed a different sense of time and space than did formerly produced designs. As pictorial narratives, the tales unfolded from one end of a cloth and culminated at the other – reaching three metres or so in length. Sequential images typically portrayed exploits of a noble warrior or the story of a fateful meeting of clans. While sometimes echoing clan histories told through ritual speech, these woven narratives also suggested an altered conceptual world of a generation of Sumbanese educated in public schools, literate and self-conscious of its own culture and history (through specific time periods) in a world context. Thus, a new genre in textiles surfaced in eastern Sumba, with profound implications regarding changes in local life and thought.

The narrative hinggis are immensely popular with tourists, in the accessibility of their meanings in heroic tales through time. These cloths have not replaced older designs in their indigenous uses and values, and are still regarded by most eastern Sumbanese as eccentric inventions toward an outside market. They are worn on occasion by local people, however, and a burial I attended near Waingapu in 1993 incorporated one such cloth.

The design maverick widely credited by local people with the initial invention of this style of fabric has also worked over the years as a tourist guide and textile agent. He has travelled to Bali and Java to sell cloth in cosmopolitan centres and has hosted numerous foreigners in his village home. In Western clothes such as T-shirts and denim jeans, he appears at ease socializing with tourists. At the same time, he is wary of the powers of local sorcery (and a professed adherent to the Marapu belief system) and plans his periodic commercial ventures away from the island by first killing a chicken and examining its entrails. He is an eastern Sumbanese partaking of a number of worlds – juggling the local with the global in his self-presentation and in the cloth he continues to design.

While a gendered difference in mobility and activity is still the norm on Sumba, women have begun to enter the commercial textile arena in recent years, with the expanded social networks and travel this implies. In some East Sumbanese villages transformations are emerging, not only in the designs and destinations of woven fabrics, but also in the social interactions and identities surrounding them. This is beginning to affect gendered roles and images in Sumbanese society. A posture of entitlement assumed in the unfettered travels of men has recently been challenged by a few enterprising women, who now follow their own travel routes, carrying textiles around the island and beyond. Moreover, tensions arise from transgressions of conventional gendered behaviour, adding further animation and intrigue to East Sumbanese social life, as gossip and resentment, as well as admiration and emulation, follow the paths of these women entrepreneurs.

In the 1990s, some eastern Sumbanese women were beginning to prosper as not only creators of cloth, but as traders. In former times, it was unheard of for a woman to set out on an enterprise of her own that involved travel away from her village to distant areas. Although it is still against the grain of proper female behaviour, some women have succeeded in bending or circumventing these conventions. One unmarried trader in her thirties had established a complex circuit of trade links throughout East Sumba by 1990. She avoided the censure of her kin by staying at relatives' homes in various regions and going out in the company of a younger female cousin. Her trade stops included tourist shops in the main town of Waingapu, as well as a number of hotels.

Another village woman went much further afield and carried boxes of fabrics made by herself and her neighbours to regions of Bali and Java. Born into the lower caste (ata) in eastern Sumba, this woman's travels and successes were inevitably followed by rumours of witchcraft and immorality. Nonetheless, she has prospered to the point of attaining a formerly unimaginable standard of living for herself in Sumba and, at least at the time of writing, contin-

Overleaf:
Page 48: Nobleman.
Page 49: Noblewomen.

ues to defy her critics by her ongoing enterprise and international contacts. While moving well beyond the boundaries of conventional society, these same women often guard the designs and quality of their pieces. It is partially through their efforts that high-quality fabrics are surfacing amidst the thousands of shoddy tourist cloths (hemba turis) being produced in the region. In fact, these female entrepreneurs often will not sell to local merchants, for fear of losing control over their designs, but instead market their cloth directly to foreigners. One woman has maintained connections with a European gallery owner since the mid-1980s, and regularly receives brochures and catalogues from exhibits abroad by mail. Significantly, the pictures from these foreign publications (including arts from across Asia) that most influenced her were those of old eastern Sumbanese royal fabrics. She has copied meticulously from these illustrations sent from Europe and now creates such fabrics anew.

Above: One of the many 'ethnic art' shops in Kuta Beach, Bali, selling Sumbanese textiles along with arts from islands across the Indonesian archipelago.
Page 50: Textiles displayed in an eastern Sumbanese village to attract the attention of incoming tourists.

Conclusion

As the design fields of eastern Sumbanese textiles have opened up in recent years, so have the routes and connections of their trade. Yet a new circularity is implied through all of these transitions. Exchange circles and fabric designs now incorporate the international world more than ever before. But they remain circles nevertheless, in which influences and people move out and back, and continue the flux and spirited competition surrounding textiles and local life. As people in eastern Sumba become more entangled in a world economy, they will also feel its surges and recessions. While the current global demand for Sumbanese fabrics may plummet, the importance of textiles in local life will carry on in some form. Weaving into the 21st century, Sumbanese fabrics will reveal other stories, shifts, and surprises in continuously unfolding passages.

Sumbanese textiles

Alit Djajasoebrata and Linda Hanssen

The making of Sumba cloth

Based on their patterning technique, East Sumba cloths can be divided into three categories. The best known are the *ikats* (all of the warp ikat type). A second group is formed by plain cloths, which are dyed after weaving and decorated with beads and embroidery. The third category consists of cloths with patterns formed by supplementary warps.

The man's sarongs are called *hinggis*, and in most cases these belong to the ikat category. In some cases they are plain undecorated cloths without patterns.

The women's sarong is called *lau*. The lau shows an abundance of embellishments. Shell and bead embroidery in large human and animal figures, sewn on *katipa*, fine woven beadbands, tufted embroidery in supplementary yarn, and surface staining in yellow and brown are used separately or in combination. According to the decoration technique, lau are divided into two categories. *Lau pahudu* is the name for the women's sarong with supplementary warps. It may be combined with stripes, ikat patterns and sewn-on bands of fringes. Women's sarongs decorated with shells and beads are called *lau hada*. At the sides they often show zoomorphic figures, formed by dark twined yarn embroidered in a tufted way, resembling a fringe.

Both East and West Sumba cloths are produced in plain weave with a warp rib on a backstrap loom without a comb.

The hinggi consists of two identical warp ikat decorated cloths, sewn together lengthwise with a Z shape stitch. Ikat cloths for hinggi are further decorated with plied and twisted ikat fringes and *kabakil*, twined or woven endborders. These characteristic narrow endborders are woven or twined into the fringes of the cloth after weaving and sewing the two pieces into one cloth. Weaving in weft-wise rib is done on a special small loom, using the warps of the ikat as the wefts of the kabakil (woven border in weft-wise rib). The warps consist of different colours or ikat yarns, which create the fine designs.

For the lau, two pieces of cloth are sewn together into a tubular form. In general the cloth is woven in one piece with different upper and lower parts, cut in half and sewn together, first along the selvages and then along the cut sides. Some of the lau however, where supplementary warp and ikat tech-

Above: tie-dyed ikat warp, Sumba, end 19th century or beginning 20th century, cotton and plant fibre, 150 cm.
Below: pattern chart, Melolo, East Sumba, c. 1930, palmleaf nerves, cotton yarn and wood, 53.6 x 50 cm.
Page 52: *hinggi*, man's mantle, Sumba, end of 19th or beginning of 20th century, plain weave, cotton, 220 x 60.5 + 60.5 cm.

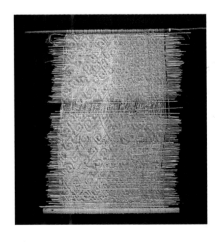

53

nique are combined, do not seem to be made from one and the same cloth, which may suggest that in some cases one woven cloth is used for more lau.

Cotton is the basic material for the cloths produced on Sumba. Until the end of the 19th century, only handspun native yarn was used, but later this was often combined with imported machinespun yarn. Contrasting import yarn in bright shades was applied for the woven fringed edges of the hinggi.

In the striped upper parts of the lau, imported and coloured yarn often prevails, whilst for the lower part homespun cotton was frequently employed. The supplementary yarns are always handtwined and handspun. For some lau hada, imported machine woven cotton cloth is even used as the foundation for embroidered beadwork. Glass beads were imported from Holland until 1920.

Most coloured cloths have been treated with natural dyes. The traditional red colour was obtained from *kombu*, the bark of the Morinda tree, and the blue from indigo. After tying the yarns into the desired patterns, they are first dipped into indigo, then into kombu. To obtain the desired red shade over the blue indigo takes many dye-baths. This results in a great variety of blues and reds. All cloths in which Morinda red is used are named after the red colour: *lau kombu* and *hinggi kombu*.

The colour of the weft varies according to the desired effect: if the main colour of the cloth has to result in a dark, deep indigo blue, the weft might be saturated in indigo as well. But if the overall colour has to be brighter and lighter, the weft might maintain its original natural hue, or undergo a colouring bath to stress the shade of the warp.

Apart from the light or dark blue and red colour combinations, bright red, yellow and orange colours were popular in the beginning of the 20th century. Additional decoration is applied by small spots of yellow and brown after the cloths are sewn together. This is achieved by staining some dyed areas, creating various effects in colours.

Decorative motifs

People of East Sumba perceive the designs in the colourful luxury cloths as symbols of royal prestige. The royal class has a significance reaching far beyond their secular role. The ruler was and still is also considered a direct heir of a great Deity who, with his servants and noble companions, descended from the heavens to the isle of Sumba, bringing the complex and rigid rules by which the society is ordered. People regard the traditional ruler with awe and fear, as a mortal possessed of super-human powers.

By way of analogy special qualities of phenomena such as large size, unusual features, or high degree of complexity are signs of the 'supra-ordinary powers of royalty' for the Sumbanese. Large animals sometimes are accompanied by much smaller ones, who seem to take a safe ride on the big ones, or seek shelter under them. Such images stand for the relationship between the nobility protecting the people dependent from them.

Large deer with great candelabra antlers, beautiful horses and human figures on textiles are referred to as belonging to the king. Only nobility could organize a deer hunt as part of the sacred rites of the dry season, and large upstanding headdresses were exclusive to royalty in Sumba. And it was the king who formally owned all livestock in his district, while all persons in the district would claim to be his servants. Dogs belong to the retinue of noblemen and assist their masters when they hunt.

Crocodiles and pythons are the most feared predators of the island. When a person is suddenly snatched away by a crocodile while taking a bath in the river, he is thought to have done a deed he thus is punished for. Because of their assumed power to punish a guilty man, crocodiles and pythons are seen as manifestations of the ever influential ancestors, as well as of their human representative, the king. Other animals living in the water, like lobsters, flat-fish, octopuses and shrimps are associated with after-life. They may be regarded as temporary forms assumed by ancestors.

Birds are often representations of chicken, whose entrails are consulted to read the future and will of the ancestors. Like buffaloes they serve as sacrificial animals. Buffaloes also represent wealth. Horses symbolize courage in warfare, nobility and wealth.

Important heirlooms like the golden *mamuli* are supposed to incorporate supernatural powers associated with the ancestral world of the nobles. Starlike and other ornamental motifs that are applied as overall fillings refer to the Sumbanese legend of the soul in heaven, who after its last time of dying, is rubbed to dust by Ina Kalada-Ama Kalada (grandmother-grandfather) and strewn over the earth, where it magically transforms into benefits for the family of the deceased.

In the centerfield of the cloths, certain patterns also are identified as signs of royalty. The most admired of these is the *patola ratu* design, said to be derived from the dappled lozenges of the python skin. The name and style of this design however show the influence of the Indian silk double ikated sari called *patola*. These cloths have long been imported into the western part of Indonesia where they were favoured elements of elite costume. The specked or mottled aspect of a python's skin refers to its multicolouredness, a highly valued sign of abundance that characterizes life and growth in general. Other designs which are likely inspired on motives of Indian patola cloths, are possibly also associated with the skin of the ever rejuvenating snake that is cast-

Above: *hinggi kombu*, man's mantle, Kambera, North Sumba, c. 1940, warp ikat, dabbed blue, imported cotton yarn, 239 x 66 + 66 cm.
Page 54:
Above: *lau pahudu*, woman's sarong, Sumba, end of 19th or beginning of 20th century, warp ikat and supplementary warp, imported cotton yarn, 112 x 67 + 73.5 cm.
Below: *lau hada*, woman's sarong, Lewa, Central Sumba, end of 19th or beginning of 20th century, plain weave with tufted embroidery in supplementary yarn, embroidered with *kauri* shells and glass beads, handspun cotton, 110 x 81 + 81 cm.

Above: Sumbanese girls wearing *lau hada*, c. 1960.
Below: Sumbanese nobleman dressed in *hinggis* with his two wives dressed in *lau*, c. 1960.
Page 57:
Above: Sumbanese men wearing *hinggis* on lower body and as shoulder cloths.
Below: Sumbanese dancers wearing *lau pahudu*, c. 1960.

ed off again and again, a symbol of life that continues after death.

One of the most striking motifs seen on Sumbanese textiles is that of the skull tree. The skull tree used to serve as the focus of a great religious celebration during which the heads of captured enemies were hung on its branches. Prior to Dutch administration, each royal village possessed such a skull tree.

Men depicted in Sumba textiles are often wearing *palang* (cross, Ind.). These are a kind of penis inserts traditionally common in Southeast Asia. In Indonesia these are still current with non-moslims in Borneo, Sulawesi, and in several regions in the Lesser Sunda Islands. In East Sumba it is a frenulum perforation with animal hair (horse, goat, sheep, or wild animal) in such a way, that a small brush is generated. Length and quantity of hairs may vary. Its purpose is to stimulate sexual pleasure.

Sumbanese textiles also show royal motifs with a foreign origin. Prestigious foreign imports such as Chinese porcelain was only within reach of the royalty and introduced motifs like elaborated dragons.

After Dutch forces put an end to the armed rivalry among Sumba royalty, they supported the authority of the local rulers and Sumbanese nobility came to identify themselves closely with the Dutch queen Wilhelmina (1880-1962). Sumbanese royalty treasured the Dutch official agreements, medaillons of honour and coins, all of which were adorned with versions of heraldic lions. The rampant lion, originating from the Dutch coat of arms became a motive in Sumbanese textile.

Among other motives that inspired the weavers have been the foreign ships, loaded with commodities that visited the island. Tall Dutch soldiers in uniform, with their shoes, strange looking caps, and shouldering rifles must have caused astonishment. As did the Dutch administrators who brought longhaired poodles with them and other dogs hitherto unknown to the Sumbanese, who called them 'Javanese dogs'. For everything new and strange was supposed to come from the west, from Java and perhaps further away.

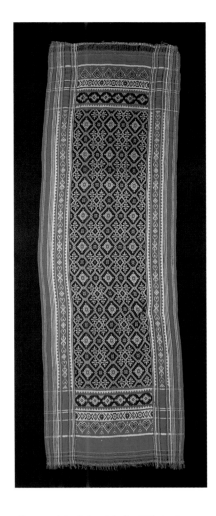

Above: *patola*, Gujerat, India, 19th century or earlier, double ikat, silk, 266 x 80 cm.
Page 60: detail of a *hinggi kombu*, man's mantle, Melolo, East Sumba, beginning of 20th century, warp ikat, cotton, 254 x 54.5 + 54.5 cm.
Page 58: detail of a *hinggi kombu*, man's mantle, Melolo, East Sumba, beginning of 20th century, warp ikat, cotton, 254 x 54.5 + 54.5 cm.
Page 59: detail of a *hinggi kombu*, man's mantle, Kapundo, North Sumba, beginning of 20th century, warp ikat, handspun cotton, kabakil and imported yarn, 245 x 53 + 53 cm.

Left: *lau*, woman's sarong, Kodi, West
Sumba, end of 19th or beginning of 20th
century, embroidery in chainstitch (dyed),
cotton and imported cloth, 118 x 85.5 cm.
Right: *lau*, woman's sarong, Kodi, West
Sumba, end of 19th or beginning of 20th
century, embroidery in chainstitch, cotton
and plain cotton fabric (dyed), 136 x 85.5 cm.
Page 62: *Lau*, woman's sarong, Kodi, West
Sumba, end of 19th or beginning of 20th
century, embroidery in chainstitch, cotton,
138 x 69.5 cm.

Left: *lau hada*, woman's sarong, Central
Sumba, end of 19th or beginning of 20th
century, plain weave, embroidered beadwork, twined fringe and twined beadwork,
imported cotton yarn and imported cotton
cloth, glass beads, 120 x 56 cm.
Right: *lau hada*, woman's sarong, Central
Sumba, end of 19th or beginning of 20th
century, warp ikat and supplementary warp,
beadwork and embroidery, knotted fringe,
cotton and glass beads, 126 x 79 + 82 cm,
beadwork 42 cm.
Page 64: *lau hada,* woman's sarong, Sumba,
end of 19th or beginning of 20th century,
plain weave and tufted embroidery with
supplementary warp, cotton, glass and
beads (attached with twined beadband),
124 x 80 + 80 cm.

Lau, woman's sarong, Central Sumba,
early 20th century, supplementary warp,
tufted embroidery with supplementary
yarn, handspun cotton, 138 x 87 + 68 cm.

Lau pahudu, woman's sarong, Sumba,
end of 19th or beginning of 20th century,
warp ikat, supplementary warp, twined
fringes, cotton, 130 x 71 + 81 cm.

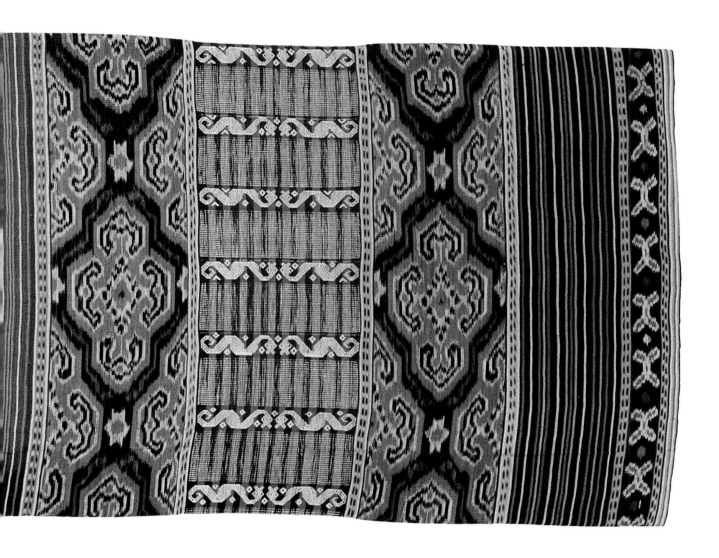

Lau pahudu, woman's sarong, Rende,
East Sumba, end of 19th or beginning
of 20th century, warp ikat, supplementary
warp, cotton, 126 x 89 + 89 cm.

Above: *lau*, woman's sarong, Sumba, end of 19th or beginning of 20th century, warp ikat, surface stained in brown, handspun cotton, 130 x 83.5 + 82 cm.

Below: *lau pahudu*, woman's sarong, East Sumba, end of 19th or beginning of 20th century, warp ikat and supplementary warp, cotton, handspun and imported yarn, 125 x 74.5 + 68 cm.

Page 70: *lau pahudu*, woman's sarong, East Sumba, first quarter of 20th century, warp ikat and supplementary warp, handspun cotton, 121 x 80 + 70 cm.

Overleaf: fragment of a *lau pahudu*, woman's sarong, Sumba, c. 1930, warp ikat and supplementary warp, cotton, 107 cm x 26.5 cm.

Left: *lau pahudu*, woman's sarong, Sumba,
end of 19th or beginning of 20th century,
warp ikat and supplementary warp, cotton,
handspun and imported yarn (bright red
and yellow), 120 x 85 + 77 cm.
Right: *lau*, woman's sarong, Sumba,
beginning of 20th century, warp ikat,
cotton, handspun and imported yarn,
132 x 71 + 67 cm.
Page 74: *lau pahudu*, woman's sarong,
Sumba, end of 19th or beginning of 20th
century, warp ikat and supplementary warp,
handspun cotton, 136 x 66 + 76 cm.

Hinggi kombu, man's mantle, East Sumba,
end 19th century or beginning 20th century,
warp ikat, cotton, handspun warp and
imported weft, 229 x 58 + 58 cm.

Hinggi kombu, man's mantle, Melolo, East Sumba, first quarter of 20th century, warp ikat, handspun cotton, 241 x 67 + 67 cm.

Hinggi kombu, man's mantle, East Sumba,
end of 19th or beginning of 20th century,
warp ikat, imported cotton yarn,
244 x 58 + 58 cm.

Left: *hinggi kombu*, man's mantle, East
Sumba, end of 19th century, warp ikat,
handspun cotton, blue dabbed warp and
imported weft, 235.5 x 60 + 60 cm.
Right: *hinggi*, man's mantle, Mangili or
Waijelo, East Sumba, beginning of 20th
century, warp ikat, cotton, handspun and
imported yarn, 230.5 x 59.5 + 59.5 cm.

Hinggi kombu, man's mantle, Taimanu,
North Sumba, end of 19th or beginning
of 20th century, warp ikat, cotton,
250 x 62.5 + 62.5 cm.

Hinggi kombu, man's mantle, Taimanu,
North Sumba, end of 19th or beginning
of 20th century, warp ikat, cotton,
262 x 59 + 59 cm.

Hinggi, man's mantle, East Sumba, c. 1940,
warp ikat, cotton (warp: imported yarn,
weft: handspun), 280 x 65 + 65 cm.

Left: *hinggi kombu*, man's mantle, East Sumba, end of 19th or beginning of 20th century, warp ikat, cotton, 280 x 60 + 60 cm.
Right: *hinggi kombu*, man's mantle, Central Sumba, end of 19th or beginning of 20th century, warp ikat, handspun cotton, 224 x 50 + 50 cm.

Hinggi kombu, man's mantle, East Sumba,
end of 19th or beginning of 20th century
warp ikat, cotton, 248 x 57 + 57 cm.

Above: *hinggi kombu*, man's mantle,
East Sumba, end of 19th or beginning of
20th century, warp ikat, handspun cotton,
296 x 54.5 + 54.5 cm.
Overleaf: *hinggi*, man's mantle, East Sumba,
c. 1940, warp ikat, handspun cotton,
152.5 x 57 + 57 cm.

Hinggi, man's mantle, Rende, East Sumba,
end of 19th or beginning of 20th century,
warp ikat, imported cotton yarn and
goldthread (in *kabakil*), 238 x 52.5 + 52.5 cm.

Left: *hinggi kombu*, man's mantle, Melolo, East Sumba, end of 19th or beginning of 20th century, warp ikat, cotton, 242 x 61 + 61 cm.
Overleaf:
Page 92: detail of a *hinggi kombu*, man's mantle, Central Sumba, beginning of 20th century, warp ikat, handspun cotton, 233 x 67 + 67 cm.
Page 93: detail of a *hinggi kombu*, man's mantle, Sumba, beginning of 20th century, warp ikat, handspun cotton, commercial cloth, 295 x 59 + 59 cm.

Left: *hinggi kombu*, man's mantle, Kambera, North Sumba, end of 19th or beginning of 20th century, warp ikat, cotton, 161 cm x 62 + 62 cm.

Right: *hinggi kombu*, man's mantle, Melolo, East Sumba, end of 19th or beginning of 20th century, warp ikat, cotton, 265 cm x 63 + 63 cm.

Page 94: *halenda kombu*, woman's shoulder strap, East Sumba, end of 19th or beginning of 20th century, warp ikat, cotton, handspun and imported yarn, 227 x 58.5 + 58.5 cm.

Page 96: *hinggi*, man's mantle, Melolo, East Sumba, end of 19th or beginning of 20th century, warp ikat, handspun cotton, 220 x 64 + 64 cm.

Page 97: *hinggi kombu*, man's mantle, East Sumba, c. 1940, warp ikat, imported cotton yarn, warp 234.5 x 65 + 65 cm.

Hinggi kombu, man's mantle, East Sumba,
end of 19th or beginning of 20th century,
warp ikat, cotton, 242 x 61 + 61 cm.

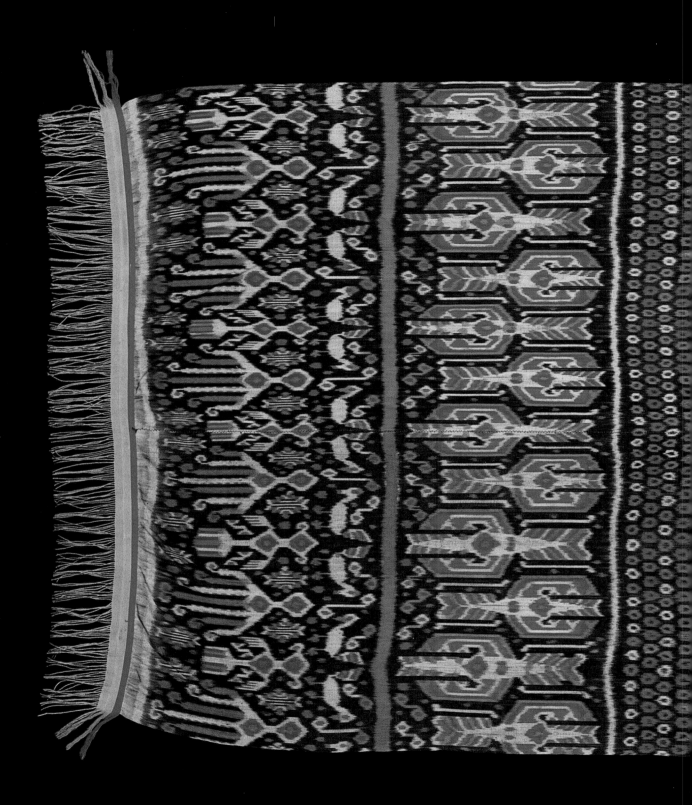

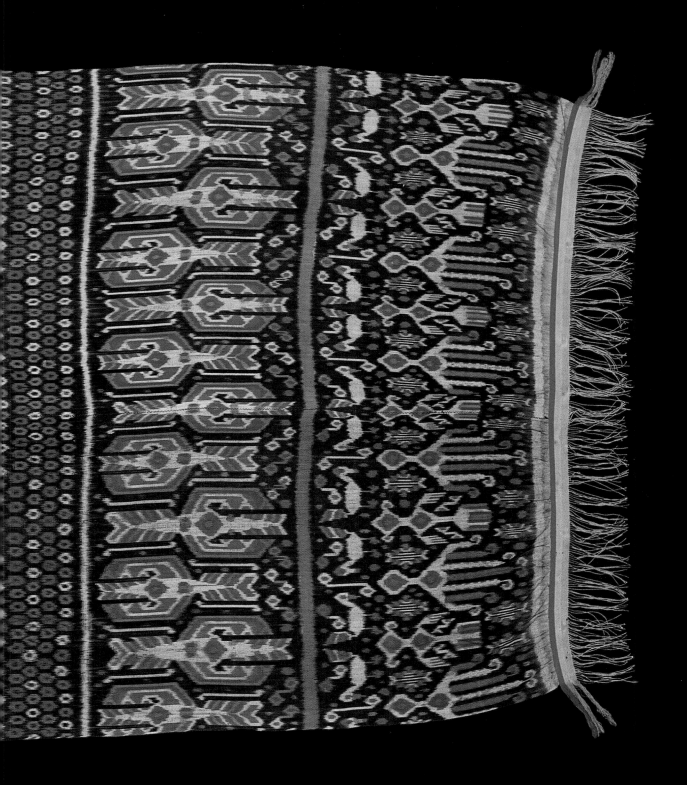

Hinggi, man's mantle, North Sumba, end of
19th or beginning of 20th century, warp ikat,
cotton, 258 x 63.5 + 63.5 cm.

Hinggi kombu, man's mantle, Kambera,
North Sumba, beginning of 20th century,
warp ikat, cotton, 272 x 57 + 57 cm.

Hinggi kombu, man's mantle, East Sumba,
end of 19th or beginning of 20th century,
warp ikat, cotton, 270.5 x 65 + 65 cm.

Hinggi, man's mantle, Waijelo, East Sumba,
c. 1930, warp ikat, imported cotton yarn,
233 x 60.5 + 60.5 cm.

Page 106-108: *hinggi kombu*, man's mantle,
Central Sumba, end of 19th or beginning
of 20th century, warp ikat, cotton,
245 x 63 + 63 cm.

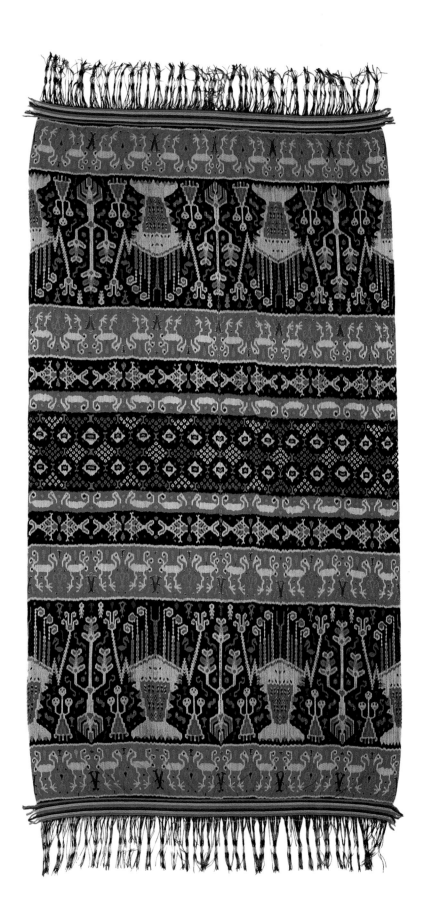

Left: *hinggi*, man's mantle, Melolo, East
Sumba, end of 19th or beginning of 20th
century, warp ikat, cotton, 285 x 62 + 62 cm.
Overleaf: *hinggi kombu*, man's mantle, East
Sumba, end of 19th or beginning of 20th
century, warp ikat, cotton, 240 x 73 + 73 cm.

Left: *hinggi kombu*, man's mantle, Sumba,
end of 19th or beginning of 20th century,
warp ikat, imported cotton yarn,
277 x 61 + 61 cm.
Right: *hinggi kombu,* man's mantle, East
Sumba, end of 19th or beginning of 20th
century, warp ikat, cotton, 262 x 61 + 61 cm.

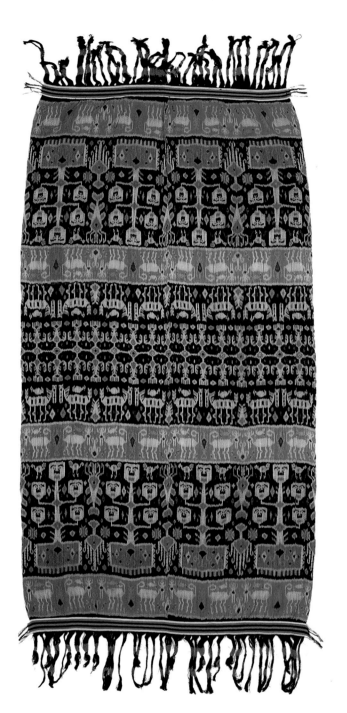 

Left: *hinggi kombu*, man's mantle, Kambera, North Sumba, end of 19th or beginning of 20th century, warp ikat, cotton, 285 x 60.5 + 60.5 cm.
Right: *hinggi kombu*, man's mantle, Kambera, North Sumba, c. 1940, warp ikat, imported cotton yarn, 279 x 64 + 64 cm.

Left: *hinggi kombu*, man's mantle,
Central Sumba, end of 19th or beginning
of 20th century, warp ikat, cotton,
291 x 61 + 61 cm.
Overleaf:
Page 116: Detail from the cloth illustrated
on page 118-119.
Page 117: Detail from the cloth illustrated
on page 123.

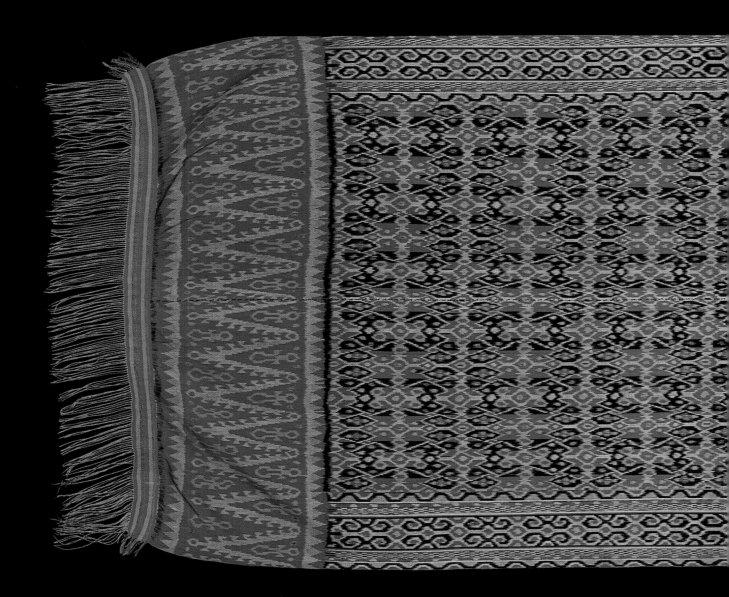

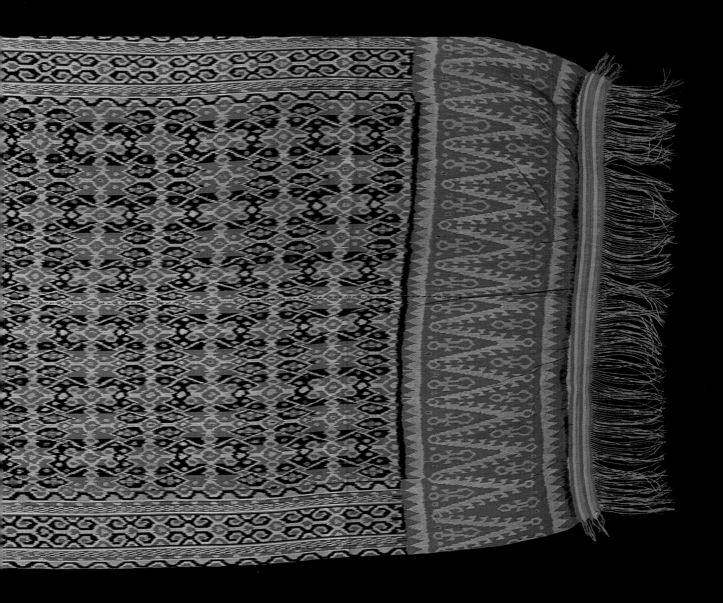

Hinggi kombu, man's mantle, East Sumba,
end of 19th or beginning of 20th century,
warp ikat, cotton, 252 x 54.5 + 54.5 cm.

Hinggi, man's mantle, Central Sumba, end of
19th or beginning of 20th century, warp ikat,
cotton, 229 x 60 + 60 cm.

Hinggi kombu, man's mantle, Central Sumba,
end of 19th or beginning of 20th century,
warp ikat, cotton, 279 x 64 + 64 cm.

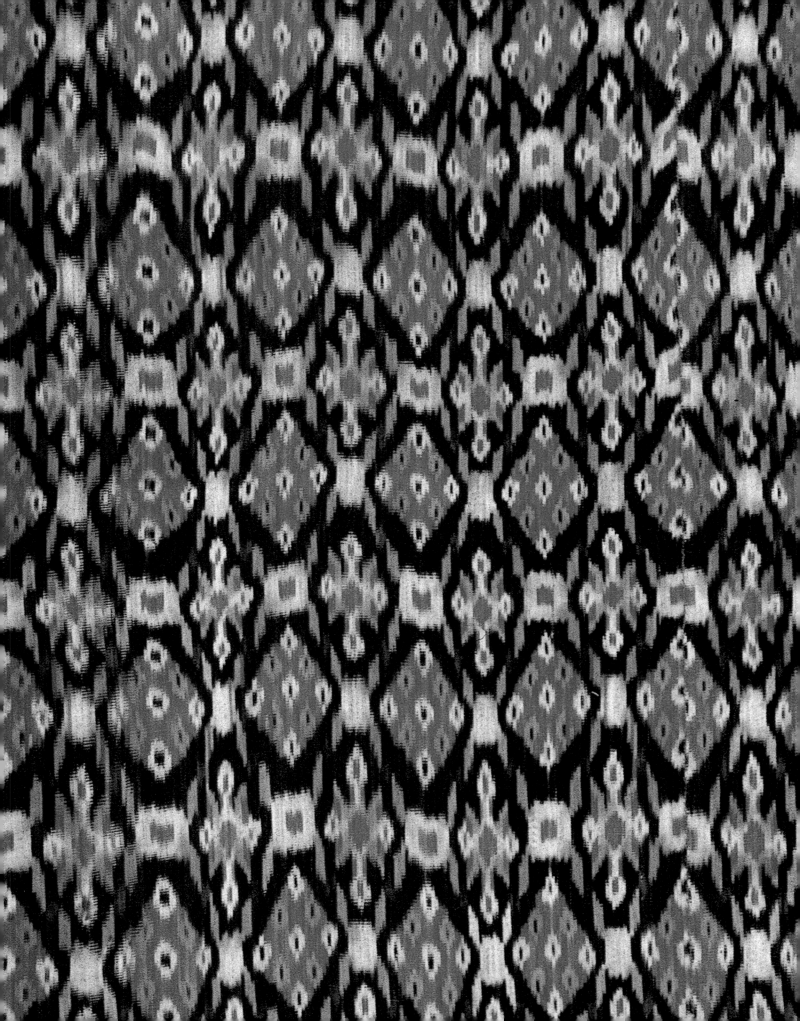

Above: *hinggi kombu*, man's mantle, East
Sumba, end of 19th or beginning of 20th
century, warp ikat, cotton, 274 x 57 + 57 cm.
Page 122: detail of a *hinggi kombu*, man's
mantle, Central Sumba, end of 19th or
beginning of 20th century, warp ikat,
cotton, 232 x 58 + 58 cm.

Hinggi kombu, man's mantle, Sumba, end of
19th or beginning of 20th century, warp ikat,
cotton, 282.5 x 66.5 + 66.5 cm.

Hinggi kombu, man's mantle, Kanatang, North Sumba, beginning of 20th century, warp ikat, cotton, 237 x 64 + 64 cm.

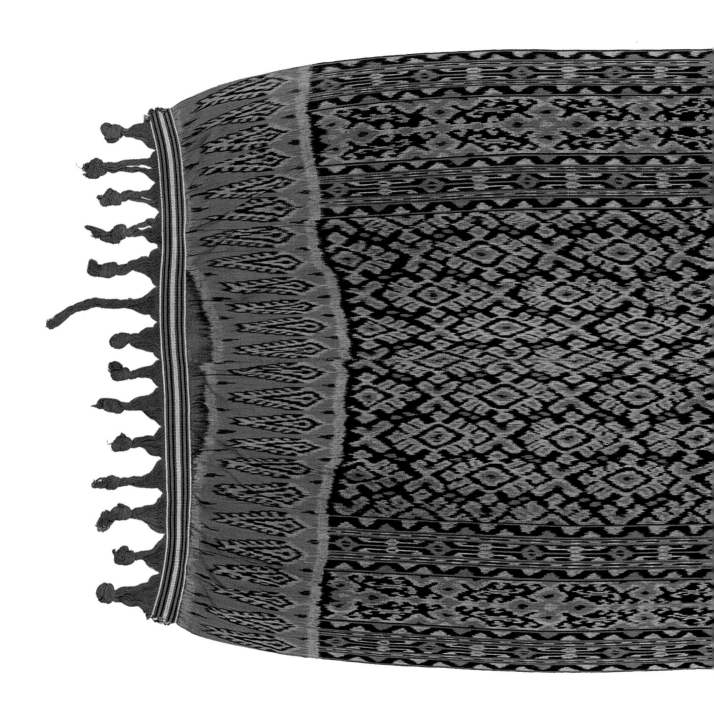

Hinggi kombu, man's mantle, East Sumba,
end 19th century or beginning of 20th
century, warp ikat and knotted fringes,
cotton, 235.5 x 62 + 62 cm.

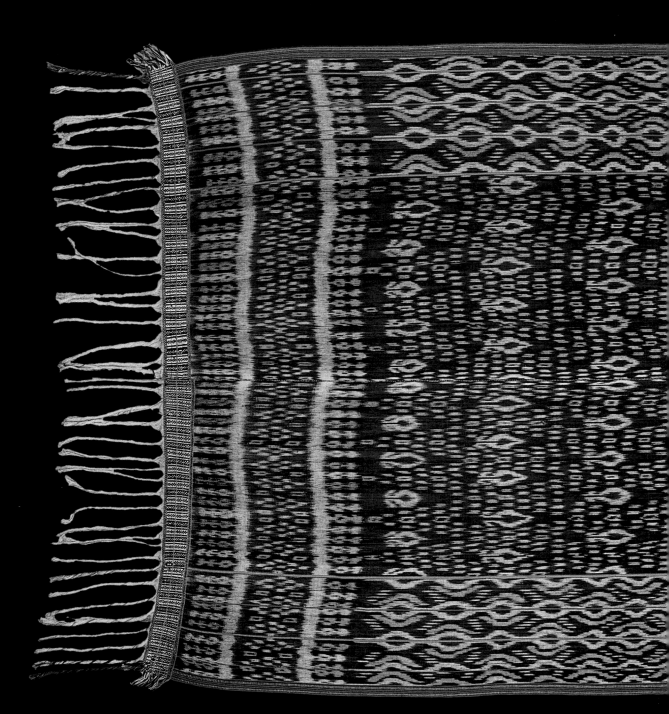

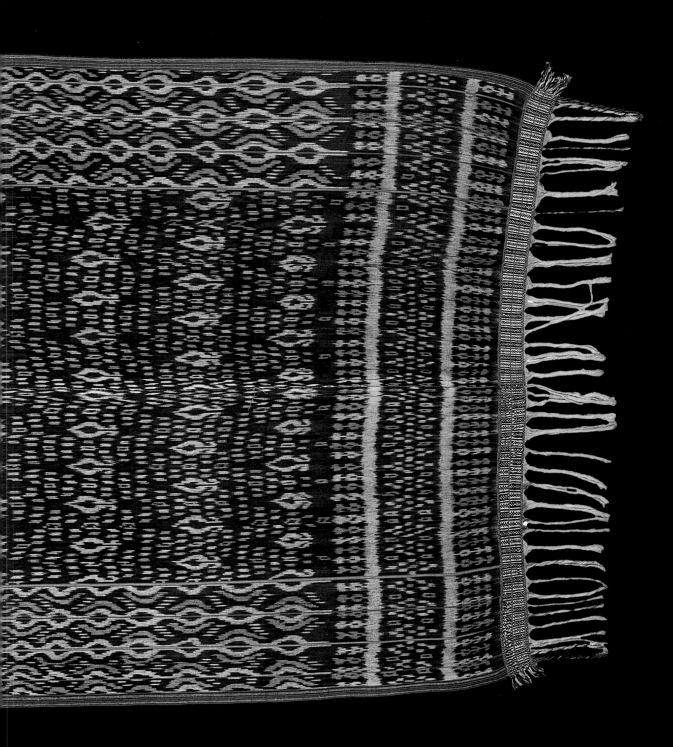

Hinggi kombu, man's mantle, Kodi, West Sumba, end of 19th or beginning of 20th century, warp ikat, handspun cotton, 140 x 66 + 66 cm.

Hinggi kombu, man's mantle, Central Sumba,
end 19th century or beginning 20th century,
warp ikat, cotton, 249 x 69 + 69 cm.

Hinggi, man's mantle, North Sumba,
end of 19th or beginning of 20th century,
warp ikat, cotton, 203.5 x 53.5 + 53.5 cm.

Above: head scarf, Sumba, warp ikat and
supplementary warp, cotton, 394 x 41 cm.
Page 132: *hinggi*, man's mantle, East Sumba,
c. 1940, warp ikat, cotton, 256 x 54 + 54 cm.

Above: *hinggi*, man's mantle, Anakalang,
West Sumba, end of 19th or beginning
of 20th century, warp ikat, cotton,
220 x 60.5 + 60.5 cm.
Page 134: *hinggi*, man's mantle,
Central Sumba, end of 19th or beginning
of 20th century, warp ikat, cotton,
239.5 x 53 + 53 cm.

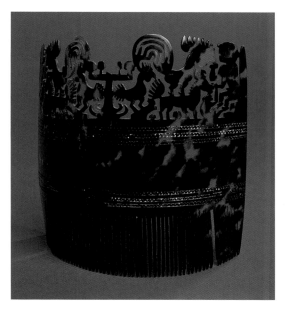 

Page 136: *hai-kara*, ornamental comb,
East Sumba, first half of 20th century,
tortoiseshell, 14 x 7 cm.
Left: *hai-kara jangga*, ornamental comb,
Sumba, first half of 20th century,
tortoiseshell and lime, 16.3 x 16.3 cm.
Right: *hai-kara jangga*, ornamental comb,
Sumba, first half of 20th century,
tortoiseshell, 17.1 x 16.4 cm.

Above: basket with lid, Sumba (possibly imported from Lampong, South Sumatra), second half of 19th century or earlier, bamboo, glass beads, cotton, cotton yarn and plant fibre, 17.5 x 26.5 x 16 cm.
Page 138: *katipa*, head ornament, Napu, North Central Sumba, end of 19th or beginning of 20th century, imported glass beads and cotton yarn, 36.8 cm x 18.5 cm.

Overleaf:
Page 140: *katipa*, beadband, Sumba, end of 19th century or beginning of 20th century, imported glass beads and cotton yarn, 134 x 15 cm.
Page 141: *katipa*, beadband, East Sumba, end of 19th or beginning of 20th century, glass, cotton yarn, imported glass beads and cotton yarn, 135.3 x 25.7 cm.

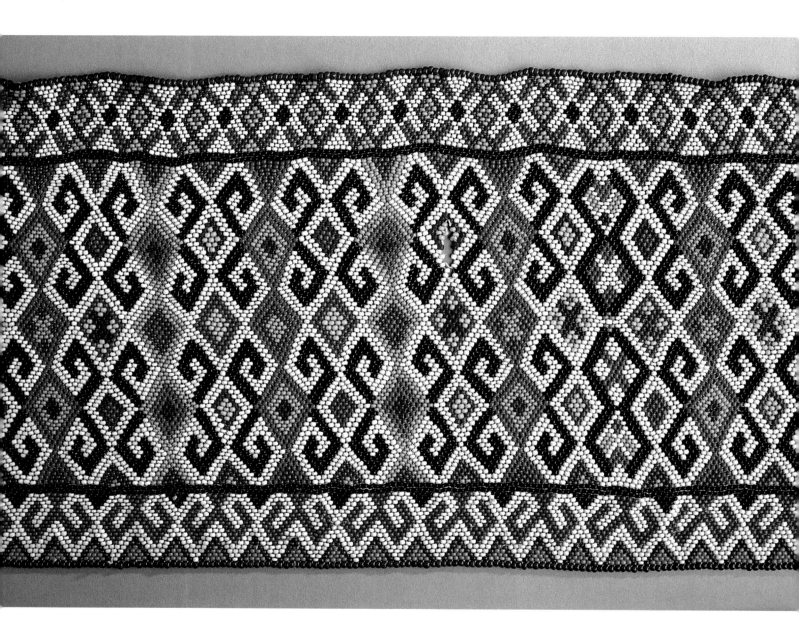

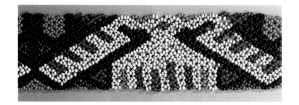

Above: *katipa*, beadband, Sumba, end of 19th or beginning of 20th century, imported glass beads and cotton yarn, 130.5 x 6.8 cm.

2nd from above: *katipa*, beadband, Sumba, end of 19th or beginning of 20th century, imported glass beads and cotton yarn, 130 x 10.8 cm.

Centre: *katipa*, beadband, Sumba, end of 19th or beginning of 20th century, imported glass beads and cotton yarn, 65.5 cm x 12.9 cm.

2nd from below: *katipa*, beadband, East Sumba, end of 19th or beginning of 20th century, imported glass beads and cotton yarn, 147 x 8 cm.

Below: *katipa*, beadband, East Sumba, end of 19th or beginning of 20th century, imported glass beads and cotton yarn, 146 x 9.5 cm.

Page 142: *katipa*, beadband, Sumba, end of 19th or beginning of 20th century, imported glass beads and cotton yarn, 108 x 10.5 cm.

Overleaf: *katipa*, beadband, Kiri Mbola, Central Sumba, end of 19th or beginning of 20th century, imported glass beads and cotton yarn, 130 x 37 cm.

Above: *katipa*, beadband, Sumba, end of 19th or beginning of 20th century, imported glass beads and cotton yarn, 140 x 7 cm.
Centre: *katipa*, beadband, Sumba, end of 19th or beginning of 20th century, imported glass beads and cotton yarn, 128.5 x 11 cm.
Below: *katipa*, beadband, Sumba, end of 19th century or beginning of 20th century, imported glass beads and cotton yarn, 170 x 10 cm.
Page 146: *katipa lunggi*, headband, Napu, North Central Sumba, end of 19th century or beginning of 20th century, imported glass beads and cotton yarn, 32 cm x 18.5 cm.

Above: box, Sumba, first half of 20th century, twined, three-line-system, lontar palmleaf, dye and cotton, 37 x 15.4 cm. Page 148: basket and lid, Sumba, first half of 20th century, twined, closed, three-line-system, lontar palmleaf.

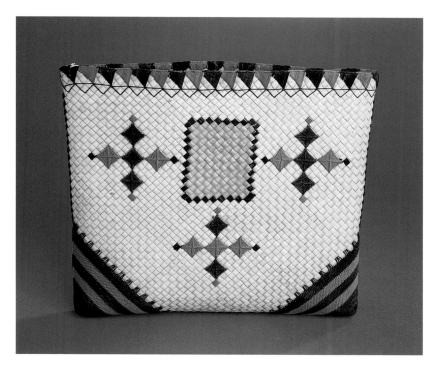

Above: *kalumbutu kaleku*, sirihbag, Sumba, first half of 20th century, twined and embroidered, palmleaf, cotton, handspun yarn, indigo dye and plant material (eye), 27.1 x 27.5 cm.

Below and page 150: *kalumbutu*, sirih bag, Sumba, first half of 20th century, twined and embroidered, lontar palmleaf, plant material, cotton, handspun yarn, and plant fibre (cord), 26.8 x 32 cm.

Page 152 and left: *tapuha*, lime gourd and
bung, Sumba, c. 1930, wood, blacking and
glass, 28.7 x 5.9 cm.
Right: *tapuha*, lime gourd and bung, Sumba,
first half of 20th century, wood and
blacking.

Notes

1 My research in Sumba took place in 1990, 1991, and 1993-1994, and was supported by the Center for Southeast Asia Studies at the University of California, Berkeley; the Fulbright Foundation; and the Wenner-Gren Foundation for Anthropological Research. Under the auspices of the Indonesian Academy of Science (LIPI), research in 1993-1994 was also sponsored by the Textile Museum in Jakarta. I thank these institutions here, and am especially indebted to the many kind Sumbanese people who inspired and enabled my study.

2 See Hoskins (1987); Keane (1996); Wielenga (1913).

3 This has been observed by many, including Adams (1969); R.H. Barnes (1974); Cunningham (1965); Forth (1981); Fox et al. (1980, 1988); Hoskins (1987, 1993); Keane (1997); Kuipers (1990); Needham (1973); Traube (1986); and Van Wouden (1968).

3 See Adams (1969); Geirnaert-Martin (1992); and Hoskins (1989) for valuable discussions of the powers ascribed to indigo in various regions of Sumba.

4 Much of the discussion in this chapter focuses upon the male garment, the *hinggi*, as opposed to the female tubular garment also produced in East Sumba, called the *lau*. *Hinggis* generally reflect innovations in Sumbanese aesthetic fields, whereas *laus* usually continue a certain conservatism in their motifs and formats. This is a trait noted by Holmgren and Spertus (1989) and relates in part to the creation of *lau* through strict reference to prior pattern guides (*pahudu*) – small sections of warp woven through with fine sticks to mark exactly how a motif should be created. The contrasting innovation and conservatism, however, between men's and women's garment designs also sug-

gests underlying differences in their worlds.

5 This is also the case in other areas of Indonesia, where marriage eligibility for women often rests on their skill at cloth production. See Barnes (1992, 1994).

6 See Adams (1969); Forth (1981); Needham (1980); Onvlee (1980b), for discussions specific to eastern Sumba, and Geirnaert-Martin (1992); Hoskins (1990); Keane (1997); and Kuipers (1990) for information regarding West Sumba. See Fox et al. (1980) for examples of exchange relations in the wider island region.

7 See Fischer et al. (1979); Gittinger (1979, 1989); Maxwell (1991). References in this brief chapter do not begin to reflect the full range of rich literature related to Indonesian cultures and textiles, but are intended to give the reader a few specific sources for further reading.

8 This is in contrast to the western part of the island, where funerals are characterized by the sacrifice of water buffaloes.

9 Adams (1969, 1971, 1972) has discussed this at length.

10 See Fischer (1979); Gittinger (1989); Hitchcock (1991); Kartiwa (1989); Langewis and Wagner (1964).

11 For examples of human figures in textiles from these regions see Fischer (1979); Hitchcock (1991); and Jacobson and Yaeger (1995).

12 This in some basic ways parallels the phenomenon called *merantau* observed by scholars throughout Indonesia, the traveling of young men to gain experience, wealth, and prestige. It is only recently, however, that such traveling for the Sumbanese (to an appreciable extent) has involved venturing away from the island.

13 See Kuipers' (1990) discussion of calamities that befall people in western Sumba who defy group norms. This nicely illustrates how exces-

sive individualism is recognized within communities and counteracted through ritual acts.

Glossary

andung skull tree

backstrap tension loom frameless loom with a backstrap, belt or wooden yoke passing around the weaver's back. At the other end of the warp another beam is held secure. The weaver controls the tension of the warp yarns by leaning forwards and backwards against the strap.

double ikat the ikat resist dyeing process applied separately to both warp and weft threads. The fabric is woven to achieve a balanced plain or tabby weave so the patterning of both sets of loom threads emerges.

hai-kara ornamental comb

halenda kombu women's shoulder strap

hinggi man's mantle

hinggi kombu man's mantle in brownish red tones, obtained from the roots of the Morinda Citrifolia

kalumbutu kaleku sirih bag

katipa beadwork border

katipa lunggi head band

ikat resist dye process, in which designs are made in warp or weft yarns. To prevent penetration of dye, small bundles of yarns are tied off with palm leaf or plastic strips. After dyeing, all resists are cut away, leaving patterned yarns ready for weaving. The process may be applied to either warp or weft yarns, or to both. In eastern Indonesia warp ikat is practiced.

kabakil endborders in weft-twined weave or in rib weave

kauri porcelain shell

kombu (*mengkudu*, Ind.) East Sumbanese name for the colour red in textiles, referring to the brownish-red colour of the Morinda-dyed yarn with the roots of Morinda Citrifolia

lau woman's sarong

lau hada woman's sarong decorated with embroidery in cotton yarn, shells and glass beads

lau pahudu woman's sarong decorated with supplementary warp.

mamuli golden female pendant

mengkudu see *kombu*

pahikung supplementary warp

palang (cross, Indon.) Penis inserts with the purpose to stimulate sexual pleasure for both partners, traditionaly common in Southeast Asia. In East Sumba it consists of a frenulum perforation with animal hair.

patola Indian double ikat cloth of silk

patola ratu ikat with 'skin of the sacred python' motif (lozenge pattern)

pote fringe, tufted embroidery or warp loop fabric for fringes in the cloth

rib weave general term used to describe weavings with strongly marked ribs. Usually when a heavier warp is covered by a fine closely packed weft, or when a fine, closely spaced warp covers a heavier weft.

supplementary warp weaving technique in which an additional set of warp threads is woven into a textile to create an ornamental pattern, additional to the ground weave.

supplementary weft weaving technique in which ornamental weft threads are woven into a textile between two regular wefts to create a pattern, additional to the ground weave.

tapuha lime gourd and bung

warp the parallel threads that run longitudinally on the loom or cloth.

weft the traverse elements in a fabric that cross and interlace with the warp and width of the cloth.

wora indigo dye, flower of the Hibiscus Rosa Sinensis

Bibliography

Adams, Marie Jeanne, *System and Meaning in East Sumba Textile Design: A Study in Traditional Indonesian Art.* Cultural Report 16. New Haven: Yale University, Southeast Asia Studies, 1969.

Adams, Marie Jeanne, 'Designs in Sumba Textiles: Local Meanings and Foreign Influence.' *Textile Museum Journal* 3:28-37, 1971.

Adams, Marie Jeanne, 'Classic and Eccentric Elements in East Sumba Textiles: A Field Report.' *Needle and Bobbin Bulletin* 55:1-40, 1972.

Barnes, Ruth, 'Without Cloth We Cannot Marry.' *Fragile Traditions: Indonesian Art in Jeopardy.* ed. Paul Michael Taylor, pp. 13-27. Honolulu: University of Hawaii Press, 1994.

Barnes, Ruth, 'Textile Design in Southern Lembata: Tradition and Change.' *Anthropology, Art, and Aesthetics*, ed. Jeremy Coote and Anthony Shelton, pp. 160-178. Oxford: Clarendon Press, 1992.

Bühler, Alfred, 'Patola Influences in Southeast Asia.' *Journal of Indian Textile History* 4:4-46, 1959.

Fischer, Joseph, *Threads of Tradition: Textiles of Indonesia and Sarawak.* Berkeley: Lowie Museum of Anthropology, University Art Museum, University of California, 1979.

Forth, Gregory, *Rindi: An Ethnographic Study of a Traditional Domain in Eastern Sumba.* The Hague: Martinus Nijhoff, 1981.

Fox, James J. (ed.), *The Flow of Life: Essays on Eastern Indonesia.* Cambridge, Mass. and London: Harvard University Press, 1980.

Geirnaert-Martin, Danielle C., *The Woven Land of Laboya: Socio-Cosmic Ideas and values in West Sumba, Eastern Indonesia.* Leiden: Centre of Non-Western Studies, Leiden University, 1992.

Geirnaert, Danielle C., *Eiland aan een draad, weefsels van Sumba.* Den Haag, Museon, 1993.

Gittinger, Mattiebelle (ed.), *Splendid symbols, Textiles and Tradition in Indonesia.* The Textile Museum. Washington D.C., 1979.

Gittinger, Mattiebelle, *To Speak with Cloth: Studies in Indonesian Textiles.* Los Angeles: Museum of Cultural History, University of California, 1989.

Hitchcock, Michael, *Indonesian Textiles.* New York: Harper Collins, 1991.

Holmgren, Robert J., and Anita E. Spertus, *Early Indonesian Textiles from Three Island Cultures: Sumba, Toraja, Lampung.* New York: The Metropolitan Museum of Art, 1989.

Hoskins, Janet, 'Entering the Bitter House: Spirit Worship and Conversion in West Sumba.' Indonesian Religions in Transition. ed. Rita Smith Kipp and Susan Rodgers, pp. 136-160. Tucson: The University of Arizona Press.

Hoskins, Janet, 'Why Do Ladies Sing the Blues? Indigo Dyeing, Cloth Production, and Gender Symbolism in Kodi.' *Cloth and Human Experience.* ed. Annette B. Weiner and Jane Schneider. Washington and London: Smithsonian Institution Press, 1989.

Hoskins, Janet, 'Doubling Deities, Descent, and Personhood: An Exploration of Kodi Gender Categories.' *Power & Difference: Gender in Island Southeast Asia.* ed. Jane Monnig Atkinson and Shelly Errington, pp. 273-306. Stanford, Ca.: Stanford University Press, 1990.

Hoskins, Janet, *The Play of Time: Kodi Perspectives on Calendars, History, and Exchange.* Berkeley, Los Angeles, and London: University of California Press, 1993.

Jacobson, Mark Ivan, and Ruth Marie Yaeger, *Traditional Textiles of West Timor: Regional Variations in Historical Perspective.* Jacksonville, Illinois: Batuan Baru Productions, 1995.

Jasper, J.E. & Mas Pirngadie, *De inlandsche kunstnijverheid in Nederlandsch Indië, Deel 1 Het vlechtwerk.* 's-Gravenhage, Boek & kunstdrukkerij v/h Mouton & Co, 1912.

Kartiwa, Suwati, *Kain Songket Indonesia: Songket Weaving in Indonesia.* Jakarta: Djambatan, 1989.

Keane, Webb, 'Materialism, Missionaries, and Modern Subjects in Colonial Indonesia.' *Conversion to Modernities: The Globalization of Christianity.* ed. Peter van der Veer. New York: Routledge, 1996.

Keane, Webb, *Signs of Recognition: Power and Hazards of Representation in an Indonesian Society.* Berkeley, Los Angeles, and London: University of California Press, 1997.

Kuipers, Joel, *Power in Performance: The Creation of Textual Authority in Weyewa Ritual Speech.* Philadelphia: University of Pennsylvania Press, 1990.

Langewis, Laurens & Frits A. Wagner, *Decorative Art in Indonesian Textiles*. Amsterdam: Van der Peet, 1964.

Maxwell, Robyn, *Textiles of Southeast Asia: Tradition, Trade, and Transformation*. Oxford: Oxford University Press, 1991.

Needham, Rodney, 'Principles and Variation in the Structure of Sumbanese Society.' *The Flow of Life: Essays on Eastern Indonesia*. ed. James J. Fox, pp. 21-47. Cambridge, Mass. and London: Harvard University Press, 1980.

Onvlee, Louis, 'The Significance of Livestock in Sumba.' *The Flow of Life: Essays on Eastern Indonesia*. ed. James J. Fox, pp. 195-207. Cambridge, Mass. and London: Harvard University Press, 1980(a).

Onvlee, Louis, 'Mannelijk en Vrouwelijk in de Sociale Organisatie van Soemba.' *Man, Meaning, and History: Essays in Honor of H.G. Schulte Nordholt*. ed. R. Schefold, J.W. Schoorl and J. Tennekes. The Hague: Martinus Nijhoff, 1980(b).

Rassers, W.H. & H.W. Fischer, *Inleiding. Catalogus van 's Rijks Ethnographish Museum* XVII: V-IX. Leiden: Rijks Ethnographisch Museum, 1924.

Wielenga, D.K., 'Soemba Voorheen en Thans.' *Indisch Genootschap, Vergadering van 18 Februari* 1913: 121-148.

Zahorka, Herwig, 'Palang-gebrauch und seine Darstellungen – über ganz Indonesien verbreitet.' *Tribus* 39:141-152. Stuttgart: Linden-Museum, 1990.

List of illustrations

Archives of the Reformed Protestant Church,
Leusden, The Netherlands
2-3, 8, 10, 12, 14-15, 16, 17, 18, 19, 20, 21, 22, 24,
26-27, 28, 29, 56, 57

Jill Forshee
4-5, 30, 32, 33, 34-35, 36, 37, 40, 41, 42, 43, 44, 45,
46, 48, 49, 50, 51

Museum of Ethnology, Rotterdam, The Netherlands
1: MvVR 62354, donation 1973 A.G. Ouwerkerk
6: MvVR 67019, legacy Mrs J.P. Wielenga
11: MvVR
52: MvVR 19836, purchase 1912 D.K. Wielenga
53: MvVR 19904 (above), purchase 1912 D.K.
Wielenga, and MvVR 27861 (right), donation
1932 L.C. Heyting
54: MvVR 19808 (above), purchase 1912
D.K. Wielenga, and MvVR 25292 (below),
purchase 1921 D.K. Wielenga
55: MvVR 45275, purchase 1958 M.A.J. Kelling
58: MvVR 25289, purchase 1921 D.K. Wielenga
59: MvVR 25280, purchase 1921 D.K. Wielenga
60: MvVR 25289, purchase 1921 D.K. Wielenga
61: MvVR 66187, purchase 1976 F. Blok
62: MvVR 19786, purchase 1912 D.K. Wielenga
63: MvVR 19787 (left) and MvVR 19788 (right),
purchase 1912 D.K. Wielenga
64: MvVR 19785, purchase 1912 D.K. Wielenga
65: MvVR 25291 (left) and MvVR 25290 (right),
purchase 1921 D.K. Wielenga
66: MvVR 25293, purchase 1921 D.K. Wielenga
67: MvVR 19807, purchase 1912 D.K. Wielenga
68-69: MvVR 58846, purchase 1969 Boeatan
70: MvVR 38839, purchase 1955 W.J.G. van
Meurs
71: MvVR 19898 (above), purchase 1921 D.K.
Wielenga, and MvVR 19814 (below), purchase
1912 D.K. Wielenga

72-73: MvVR 74266-2, donation 1997
Mrs Klitschie-Krijger
74: MvVR 19809, purchase 1912 D.K. Wielenga
75: MvVR 19811 (left), purchase 1912 D.K.
Wielenga, and MvVR 25295 (right), purchase
1921 D.K. Wielenga
76-77: MvVR 25322, purchase 1921 D.K. van
Hardenberg
78: MvVR 25286, purchase 1921 D.K. Wielenga
79: MvVR 19857, purchase 1912 D.K. Wielenga
Dr. Forshee supposes this cloth may originate
from Payeti, but in any case not far from
Waingapu. The red spot at the throat may be a
reference to the sound of voice.
80: MvVR 34498, purchase 1954 Mrs Broek
81: MvVR 25288, purchase 1921 D.K. Wielenga
82: MvVR 19888, purchase 1912 D.K. Wielenga
83: MvVR 19875, purchase 1912 D.K.Wielenga
84: MvVR 62354, donation 1973 A.G. Ouwerkerk
85: MvVR 19859 (left) and MvVR 19863 (right),
purchase 1912 D.K. Wielenga
86: MvVR 19852, purchase 1912 D.K. Wielenga
87: MvVR 19848, purchase 1912 D.K. Wielenga
88-89: MvVR 31343, purchase 1950 Verhoeven
90: MvVR 19847, purchase 1912 D.K. Wielenga
91: MvVR 19876, purchase 1912 D.K. Wielenga
92: MvVR 26957, legacy 1928
93: MvVR 38836, purchase 1955 W.J.G. van
Meurs
94: MvVR 19853, purchase 1912 D.K. Wielenga
95: MvVR 19840 (left) and MvVR 19849 (right),
purchase 1912 D.K.Wielenga
96: MvVR 19892, purchase 1912 D.K. Wielenga
97: MvVR 65139, donation 1976 T. Jansen
98-99: MvVR 19856, purchase 1912
D.K. Wielenga
100-101: MvVR 7566, purchase 1922 F. Fokkens
102-103: MvVR 25284, purchase 1921
D.K. Wielenga
104: MvVR 19854, purchase 1912 D.K. Wielenga

105: MvVR 49557, donation 1959 L.C. Heyting
106-108: MvVR 19885, purchase 1912 D.K.
Wielenga
109: MvVR 19882, purchase 1912 D.K. Wielenga
110-111: MvVR 19874, purchase 1912
D.K. Wielenga
112: MvVR 19868 (left) and MvVR 19877 (right),
purchase 1912 D.K. Wielenga
113: MvVR 19873b (left), purchase 1912 D.K.
Wielenga, and MvVR 45274 (right), purchase
1958 M.A.J. Kelling
114-115: MvVR 19864, purchase 1912
D.K. Wielenga
116: MvVR 67018, legacy 1979 Mrs J.P. Wielenga
117: MvVR 19858, purchase 1912 D.K. Wielenga
118-119: MvVR 67018, legacy 1979 Mrs J.P.
Wielenga
120: MvVR 19878, purchase 1912 D.K. Wielenga
121: MvVR 19869, purchase 1912 D.K. Wielenga
122: MvVR 19838, purchase 1912 D.K. Wielenga
123: MvVR 19858, purchase 1912 D.K. Wielenga
124: MvVR 19884, purchase 1912 D.K. Wielenga
125: MvVR 25281
126-127: purchase 1921 D.K. Wielenga and
MvVR 17406, purchase 1955 N.Z.G. (Dutch
Protestant Missionary Society)
128-129: MvVR 19894, purchase 1921
D.K. Wielenga
130: MvVR 25321, purchase 1921 D.K. van
Hardenberg.
131: MvVR 7565, purchase 1922 F. Fokkens
132: MvVR 45273, purchase 1958 M.A.J. Kelling
133: MvVR 26559, purchase 1928
134: MvVR 19833, purchase 1912 D.K. Wielenga
135: MvVR 19836, purchase 1912 D.K.Wielenga
136: MvVR 21299, purchase 1931 D.K. Wielenga
137: MvVR 21297 (left), purchase 1931 D.K.
Wielenga and MvVR 49554 (right), donation 1959
C. Goedhart

138: MvVR 25314, purchase 1921 D.K. Wielenga

139: MvVR 24724, donation 1920 G.P. Rouffaer:
'through mediation of Lt. C.A. Rijnders I bought
these two head ornaments [MvVR 24724 and
MvVR 24723] in Napu for Dfl. 12.50 at the occasion of the ritual application of the covering
stone on the Raja's grave.'

140: MvVR 25700, purchase 1921 D.K. Wielenga

141: MvVR 67024, legacy 1979 Mrs J.P. Wielenga

142: MvVR 25308, purchase 1921
D.K. Wielenga

43: (from top to bottom) MvVR 25306, MvVR
19912, MvVR 25301, MvVR 19915, MvVR 25296,
purchase 1921 D.K. Wielenga

144-145: MvVR 25305, purchase 1921 D.K.
Wielenga

146: MvVR 24723, donation 1920 G.P. Rouffaer

147: MvVR 25302 (above), MvVR 25304 (centre)
and MvVR 25303 (below), purchase 1921 D.K.
Wielenga

148: MvVR 21358, purchase 1931 D.K. Wielenga

149: MvVR 21359, purchase 1931 D.K. Wielenga

150: MvVR 21348, purchase 1931 D.K. Wielenga

151: MvVR 21350 (above) and MvVR 21348
(below), purchase 1931 D.K. Wielenga

152: MvVR 34499 (left), purchase 1954 Mrs Broek
and MvVR 21264 (right), purchase 1931 D.K.
Wielenga

Index